FOREVER AND EVER

STEVE CAWLEY

S☀CCIONES

ISBN: 9798575323181

Typesetting & cover design by Socciones Editoria Digitale
www.socciones.co.uk

CONTENTS

INTRODUCTORY NOTES ON THE TEXT

After an Introductory chapter explains how my devotion to United came about there follows seven chapters over a time period from 1964 to 1984. These chapters focus on some of the magical names and matches that played a significant part both in my growing support for the 'Reds' and in the illustrious history of the football club.

The format of the main chapters follows a similar template, with a photograph that places 'In the Picture' players, managers or matches that were of particular significance to the author. This photograph is then placed in the wider context, 'The Bigger Picture' of what was happening to United during this time period. This section will also include a brief statistical summary of the various managers at the club during this time period, what their teams achieved, their most expensive player purchased and the most significant youth player who made his debut under that manager. This last point is very important to United fans, who take great pride in a youth system that has been an integral part of the club's culture. The club is truly unique in having a home-grown product in the first team squad for over 4,000 consecutive matches; a run that goes back over an incredible eighty-three years.

Finally, a brief reference is made to modern day United managers, as there are some uncanny parallels with modern happenings at United with the events of many years ago.

Although the statistical section is relatively self-explanatory some competition abbreviation is used and the key for this is as follows:

EC: European Cup

ICFC: Inter-Cities Fairs Cup

UEFA: Union European Football Associations

ECWC: European Cup Winners Cup

EL: Europa League

CL: Champions League

Qualify: Qualifying Round

Rel: Relegated

Champ: Champions

1

BEGINNINGS

'My old man said be a City fan', goes the Man United fans' chant about a fate worse than death. Apparently, that is ending up being a supporter of City, rather than their beloved United. Well, my 'old man' didn't say that at all. In fact, he would have seen supporting a football team, to be a total waste of his hard-earned money, and he was much happier sending it in the direction of Mancunian public houses! My devotion to United for well over fifty years would have been beyond his comprehension, but from my standpoint, it has always made life worthwhile. What is a fan? The Oxford dictionary tells us that it is, 'a person who supports a particular football team'. It is, of course, a lot more than that. The word fan is clearly derived from fanatic. Keep going down that linguistic line and I'm sure you could come out with a term like insane! However exaggerated that term might be, it could have a certain application as you might have to be insanely loyal to 'your' team, because along with all the glory there will always be misfortune that can affect your team; both on the playing field and off it. Loyalty is the key component for the genuine football fan. You support your team through thick and thin. This reinforces the tie that exists between you and your club. The genuine football fan obsessively watches his team's games, reads all those newspaper reports, knows the club's history inside out and will therefore be knowledgeable enough to talk about the club and its fabled past. These things cannot be gained by a quick flit through the social websites and gossip columns, it is earned over time, and once attained it lasts, as the chant says, 'for ever and ever'. The great Sir Matt Busby (or was it Jock Stein?) famously said that 'Football is nothing without fans'. That theory is being sorely tested by COVID-19, but in a strange way, watching those unusual games in those ghostly empty stadiums emphasises the point.

I suppose looking back on it now, it was my big brother Ray that I have to thank for sowing those first seeds of interest that grew into a lifetime passion. He influenced my initial interest in the beautiful game, and in particular it was his collection of old football annuals from the late fifties that fired my imagination. As a sickly child growing up in sixties Manchester, these annuals proved a welcome distraction as I recovered from the latest ailment that seemed common for young children of that time; be it measles or mumps. Those annuals opened up a vista of dreams and aspirations that would be more than fulfilled in a lifetime of support for the 'Reds'. The books had a standard format in that they recorded the previous seasons highlights, usually the FA Cup winners, League champions and that other staple of a less globalised football calendar, The Home International Championship. Usually, there were black and white action photographs, linked to an analysis of the seasons key moments and neatly summed up with all those league tables. However, to my juvenile eyes the pages that really stood out were the full-page illustrations in full colour of various football stars. These were not photographs but a form of artist impression, in garish bright colours of various players in static pose. They appeared to be technicolour inserts into the black and white world of 1950's football.

It was while thumbing through the 1958 Football Champions annual, during one such illness bout, that I came across a picture that grabbed my immediate attention, because it was so different to anything else in the book. Instead of an action shot of a diving goalkeeper, or the net bulging with a rasping shot, this was a black and white picture of the shattered nose and fuselage of an aeroplane. The eerie photograph showed three individuals who clearly were not footballers, but appeared to be policeman standing guard, and snowflakes appeared to be falling. It was of course the BEA Elizabethan airliner that had crashed at Munich airport while taking off with the United team onboard. This was about five years after the horrific crash, but nobody had told me about this tragedy, so I had to read the page entitled 'Manchester United rise again', to try to make sense of what had happened. Even to a young boy it didn't take long to grasp the magnitude of the event. The destruction of United's youthful champions, the 'Busby babes', with eight of their players amongst the twenty-three killed in the crash. I had gleaned that United were the dominant side in Britain through reading the earlier annuals in the collection, having won the championship for the two previous seasons. Now I was reading that eight of their players were dead, and with two players subsequently unable ever to play again, I realised that was virtually the full team. In a day before squads and substitutes this must have been a mortal blow to the very future of the football club. In the article that ran alongside the pictures the United chairman Harold Hardman's speech was quoted under the heading that United would 'rise again'. Hardman said: 'Although we mourn our dead and grieve for our wounded, we believe that great days are not done for us'. I was seven years old. I had not seen United play, but from that moment on United were my team, 'for ever and ever', as they say.

Gazing at the illustrations under the title, 'Manchester United rise again', it was difficult for a young mind to put together any sort of chronology. One picture showed the devastating effects of the plane crash, while the picture below showed a determined looking Bill Foulkes leading out a United side for a match, and the last picture showed Colin Webster scoring a vital last-minute goal. Eventually, I was able to put things together. Despite the devastation of the crash, United seemed to have continued playing and the pictures were recording some sort of improbable run to that May's FA Cup Final. The following pages illustrated the FA Cup Final, where United had played Lancashire rivals Bolton Wanderers. The phoenix-like recovery didn't seem to have had a happy ending as United appeared to have lost the Final by two goals to nil. As I read through the detail of the Final, two thoughts occurred to me. One was that although Bolton had won the game, their second goal scored by centre forward Nat Lofthouse had been a controversial one. Earlier in the annual, a double page spread was devoted to this goal under the subtitle, 'Was Lofthouse's second goal a foul?' I was clearly developing the antenna of the budding football fan by sniffing out the whiff of controversy and the fans' innate ability to spot a perceived injustice. The double page was divided into seven sequential action shots that started with the United goalkeeper grasping a high ball, but by the second photograph Bolton's burley centre-forward had appeared and over the next two shots appears to barge into the goalkeeper. As Gregg crumples to the ground, the ball is released from his grasp and rolls into the net. The Football Annual reported that Gregg is 'out' and Lofthouse 'turns in triumph'. Obviously, the mores of the time were challenged as the writer tries to justify what seems to the naked eye to be a blatant foul, by saying that although Lofthouse hasn't headed the ball, the 'rules state that there is no foul if the intention is to play the ball'. Watching the action on YouTube over sixty years later can be instructive. The first thing to note that couldn't come across in the book, is how long the stoppage was. Heavyweight boxers have come around quicker than Gregg did that day. The second was how that doyen of football commentators, Kenneth Wolstenholme, analysed the goal during this stoppage, saying 'Many people are of the opinion that Gregg was charged in the back' but that it didn't matter because, 'The referee has given the goal'.

To an impressionable young mind reading through that annual, this seemed to be the only action that mattered. It didn't concern me that Bolton were considered to have been worthy winners. There was enough doubt here about underhand methods to sully their win.

Given all that had gone before, all this did was reinforce the notion that United were the team for me. The second issue that began to get me thinking was it began to dawn on me that my big brother, who I worshiped and owed so much to, was in fact a Bolton supporter! This came out in subsequent years and was totally beyond my comprehension, as I would have thought that everybody in Manchester (maybe even City fans) were willing United to win the Cup that day. Although this didn't loosen the tight bond that existed between us, it taught me something about the contrarian nature of his personality that is evident to this day.

No, I had a lot to thank my big brother for. His paternal interest in me opened up a whole world of sport. I remember in 1964, he stayed up all night to listen to the radio, and the next day he regaled me with tales of how an unknown boxer called Cassius Clay had beaten the fearsome Heavyweight champion, Sonny Liston. In the summer, he brought me to the 'other Old Trafford', and I was introduced to a day at the test cricket, when the Australian captain, Bobby Simpson, seemed to bat for all five days to score 311. It was football I was smitten with, though, and although not a regular attender yet, a pattern to the football year had been established. In those days of the early sixties, the only football people ever saw 'live' was the FA Cup Final. Back then this was a glamorous, prestigious competition, and the most important game of the season. Not least because it was the only game televised live. However, the television was a luxury too far in our household in 1962, and so again it was my brother that brought me with him when he visited his friends on Mersey Bank to watch the Cup Final on their television sets. It was always a grand day, with ladies bustling around making a fuss of the nipper and giving me sandwiches and pop as Tottenham proceeded to win the Cup. The 'box' offered yet another magical dimension to the excitement of the 'people's game', and within a year I was amazed to find that we too were to have a television set. In perfect synchronicity, within months of the 'box' arriving, I was sitting in our own back room watching the Cup Final, and as destiny would have it, it was my heroes in red that were playing.

At that time, in May of 1963, I knew little of the team's poor season in the league that had nearly led to their relegation to division two. Life, it would seem, had been difficult for United and Busby after Munich. After an amazing season when they had defied expectations by being the League runner-up, subsequent seasons had seen the Reds drift down the league table. Little did I realise it at the time, but as I sat down to take in the wonders of my team being in the Cup Final, this was a match that would prove to be a watershed in Matt Busby's search to bring back the 'great days' that Harold Hardman had talked about five years before.

That flickering black and white screen became a purveyor of magic, as United, who were apparently underdogs against Leicester City, proceeded to put on their best show of the season and win the Cup in some style. It was Denis Law who relished this big occasion and proceeded to give a man of the match display as the England goalkeeper, Gordon Banks, sought to keep him at bay. Denis was literally everywhere as the white-shirted Leicester players struggled to pick him up as he roved all over the pitch. Even Banks was left helpless after half an hour as the Lawman took Crerand's squared pass on his instep and in a trice pirouetting to his right sent a precise shot across the goalkeeper and into the left-hand corner of the net. It was a sensational strike, and as Kenneth Wolstenholme told us he'd done it I jumped to my feet in delight. Denis was unplayable, carving the Leicester defence apart. He went around

Banks and only a goal line clearance stopped him scoring again. When, late in the game, his header flashed past Banks, it thudded against a post and rebounded straight into the goalkeeper's arms. Despite David Herd scoring twice in United's 3-1 victory, it was Denis that left a lasting impression, and not just on myself. Gordon Banks commented years later: 'He had such fast reactions in the penalty box it was as if he was plugged into the mains'. We were certainly plugged into the mains, the television 'box' had brought all those pictures in football annuals to life; I was hooked forever.

Given that this was the only 'live' action football shown on the television in those days, there had to be other means of keeping up with your favourite football team. It would be hard for today's generation - brought up with instant goal texts on their phones, wall to wall football coverage and live action of games not just here but abroad, to realise what a void us football fans lived in. Instead, it was the good old Football Pink that proved a lifeline. An offshoot of the Manchester Evening News, every Saturday night it brought us all the scores, reports, pictures and analysis, not just of United but a host of Greater Manchester football teams. The paper came out about an hour after the final whistle, and soon my regular beat was to make my way down to Bancroft's newsagents on Burton Road, just before six, and join that little band of people that waited for the van to drive by and drop the bundle of pink 'uns by the shop door. Its large-scale headline would whet the appetite for a good night's reading. It might be 'LAW NABS 3: CITY 2-4' or on that Cup Final night, 'CLASSY REDS WIN A SUPER FINAL'.

The following season of 63-64, I finally managed to persuade my brother to take me to a 'live' match at Old Trafford. To be honest, I remember virtually nothing about the game; an Easter fixture with Fulham. My overriding memory was about the atmosphere of the occasion. The excitement was palpable. It seemed to my young ears to be a cauldron of noise as we stood on the terraces. You had to move quickly as the large crowd swayed backwards and forwards, and just being able to see anything on the pitch was quite an achievement. When I did get a glimpse of the play, I could make out United's bold red shirts; luminous against a grimy background. All my football pink reading paid off too, as I was able to put a name to each of those white numbers splayed over the backs of the players. Little did I realise it then, but I was witnessing the arrival of Matt Busby's third great side, a team that would banish the horrors of Munich and restore United to the pinnacle of British and European football. This was the United of Charlton, Law and Best, a side that I would be able to see on a regular basis as they went on to win two Championships and the holy grail of the European Cup. This was some team to be a fan of, and I considered myself blessed as I entered my teenage years, sated by the glory that appeared to be United's birthright. The 1970's disabused me of such complacency as United struggled after Sir Matt Busby retired. However, when you're a fan 'for ever and ever' you have to support the team whatever the fates had in store, and by 1974, that included an impossibility; relegation to the second division. Managerial changes had become the norm as the managerial roundabout had included McGuinness, O'Farrell, Docherty, Sexton and Atkinson as they all sought to put United back to their pre-eminent position. There were glories still to be had, Cups to be won and some great players to wear the shirts. As an older man, the fan remained. Even when study or employment opportunities took me away from my hometown. United were my team and Old Trafford on a Saturday was home. By the 1990's I was even able to write some books on the Reds and much to my delight Sir Matt Busby wrote an introduction that encapsulated what being a fan of the Reds really meant: 'We could be fiercely proud of our club' he wrote 'and rightly so as they brought honour and distinction', to Manchester.

More than fifty years after attending my first football match, looking back over a set of photographs in my collection, I have put together a narrative that tells a story of this football support from those mid-sixties up to the point when a manager came down from Aberdeen and changed everything that went before. There was, though, life before Fergie, and the following chapters outline that story.

2

IN THE PICTURE

BOBBY CHARLTON & DENIS LAW

What's this? Two of United's all-time legends, Bobby Charlton and Denis Law, and they are wearing City's sky blue shirts. No, it was not a moment of wavering in my growing devotion to United, but a photograph of my two heroes with the City goalkeeper, Bert Trautman, at the time of his testimonial match in April 1964. It is also just about the first match I can ever remember attending and starting over half a century of watching and supporting Manchester United. It is all the more ironic that the picture was taken at City's Maine Road ground, as the giant keeper welcomes the two 'Reds' that will play for his Manchester eleven in the game.

Although I had been to see United in that 1963-64 season, I remembered very little about the occasion, other than the fact that Old Trafford was a noisy, lively arena and the United men ran around with those bright red shirts that shone in the murk of a dank Manchester day. All the other action, from what had been a rip-roaring season for the Reds, had been devoured from the press and in particular all those match reports in the 'Pink'.

Now, with the season drawing to a close and United's pursuit of three trophies coming to an end, I set my heart on going to this testimonial game. In the days preceding the game, it was my elder sister that I pestered into taking me to the fixture. She had a passing interest in the game and indeed had been to watch United in the immediate post-Munich seasons, so she eventually acceded to my wishes and agreed to bring her little brother to Manchester's biggest game for many a year.

It might seem strange to today's more tribalistic supporters that I was happy to attend a game at Maine road that was to celebrate the City keeper, but this particular game did not divide supporters in this way. There was a sizeable United presence in the support, there not least because half of Trautman's team were to be made up of United players and, in particular, the star turns of Denis Law and Bobby Charlton.

It is often forgotten these days that in the past there was something of a tradition of Manchester supporters taking in games at both Old Trafford and Maine Road. Certainly, United fans of an older vintage had regularly attended Maine Road, because in the immediate post-war seasons, it was the venue for their home games due to the fact that a bomb-damaged Old Trafford was out of action. United actually played at Maine Road for three full seasons, and Matt Busby's first great side, captained by Johnnie Carey and starring Mitten, Rowley and Pearson set a high standard, playing a brand of attacking, exciting and successful football that would characterise all Busby's great teams. Busby's United attracted massive audiences on a regular basis, culminating in the 83,260 people who saw United set a league record in their game against Arsenal in January 1948. City, who had the bigger attendances before the war, never saw such pre-eminence again, as many neutrals went with United when they returned to Old Trafford in 1949.

Growing up in the sixties, I knew of people that went to both grounds. Their allegiance might have been to one team, but that didn't stop them watching the other lot from time to time.

One must not become misty-eyed over this Mancunian fraternity, as it was obvious to me, even from this early age, that you were either a red or a blue. Certainly, the dramatic denouement of the previous season's derby - when United had claimed a controversial late penalty, which effectively saved their skin and relegated City - still rankled with the blue half of Manchester.

Denis Law, who had controversially won that late penalty for United, was now to be seen in the photograph smiling and joking with Trautman. Quite what the City fans made of their former player's antics was not hard to speculate on, and his reappearance here for the game probably led to mixed feelings! City had smashed the British transfer record to recruit Law from Huddersfield in 1960, but his stay at Maine Road was brief, as he joined Torino of Italy in 1961. Although, even at this early stage in his career, Law was marked out as a special talent, his spell with the blues was not a happy one. He confessed in his autobiography of his difficulties playing in a 'struggling team', candidly reflecting that, 'apart from Bert Trautman, only Ken Barnes and George Hannah could play'. Despite these problems, Law still showed glimpses of his natural goalscoring talents, none more so than when he single-handedly reversed a two-goal deficit in a Cup match at Luton by banging in six goals, only for the referee to abandon the tie due to torrential rain! The fact that City lost the re-arranged game seemed to sum up his time at the Maine Road club.

All that was history now, as Law brought 'home' by Busby in another record-breaking transfer in 1962, was United's kingpin, enjoying the greatest season of his career. He had established himself the previous season at United, scoring twenty-nine times, and his stylish goal at Wembley helped to win United the FA Cup, their first trophy since Munich. Law's characteristic swivel and crisp strike into the corner of the net defeated the great Gordon Banks and further entrenched my feeling that I was blessed to be a supporter of the Reds.

By the season of the testimonial, Law was in his absolute pomp. At the age of twenty-four he was one of the greatest players in the World, an accolade that would be formalised at the seasons end when he was named the European footballer of the year. United were enjoying a wonderful season in pursuit of a treble of the league title, the FA Cup and the European Cup-winners' Cup. Busby had finally developed a team that could live and play in the traditions of the great sides that had come before them. More than anything else, it was Law's bravado and phenomenal strike rate that was behind United's return to the higher echelons of the game. Despite not being the tallest, Law scored many brilliant headed goals, with an uncanny ability to seemingly hover in the air before heading into the corner of the net. He matched this with goals on the floor from all angles, characteristically followed by that right arm with the shirt cuff held down as it shot heavenwards, as if to emphasise the divine nature of what we were witnessing. In many senses, Denis was the first football showman; perfectly in tune with the swinging sixties, a break from all that had gone before him, but a model that all future goal-scorers would imitate.

Following the 'Lawman's' deeds, I also became aware of the volatile nature of United's star forward. He didn't take kindly to the close attentions of the rugged defenders that typified sixties football, at a time when the lethal tackle from behind had not been outlawed. He seemed to belong to the school of 'getting your revenge in first'. Denis's goals to games ratio was sensational in this season, and this was important because it was soon obvious that either injury or suspension would rob Busby of his most potent weapon. Rumour was established this particular season that the "King", as he would be famously known, would time any such misbehaviour to coincide with December. This was so that by the time he was sentenced to a suspension it would coincide with the new year, and so that as a proud Scotsman he could enjoy Hogmanay back in Scotland!

This appeared to be the case to my juvenile eyes as I recorded the season, match by match. The quicksilver Scot had got United off to a terrific start to the campaign, where he appeared to resist scoring individual match goals, but usually dealt in doubles, or more often, hat-tricks; of which he scored an amazing seven over the season. He started the season with a burst of eight goals in six matches, which fired United to the top of the league, before injury stopped his march. He marked his return in October by smashing a hat-trick in the European Cup Winners' Cup. I have a vague memory of seeing what he could do, as my brother had the novel idea of bringing me to a game and just entering the ground for the last twenty minutes when the gates opened, and it was free! Law, was in his element and although, I didn't actually see it. he had astonished the home crowd by scoring an audacious headed goal from a grounded position. It was in the following game, though, that Denis's demons came to the surface, and he was sent off for retaliation in a heavy defeat at Aston Villa, The Football Pink summed up the 'disaster' as the 'fiery, brilliant United forward was sent off'. Needless to say, with a swingeing twenty-eight-day suspension set for Christmas and New Year, Denis signed off with a sensational four goals against Stoke. The papers were full of the draconian suspension, with the mores of the day dictating that ill-discipline should be penalised heavily as an example, no doubt to gullible young spectators like myself! My own view was that it was an outlandishly severe suspension that robbed United of their talisman for many games, while the arbitrary defensive thuggishness that was commonplace went unchecked.

On the Lawman's return, normal service was resumed. Denis's goals had United on the assent as further goals against Spurs, had the Reds just behind the league leaders with games in hand. In Europe, United were going great guns, having already eliminated Spurs from the competition, yet another Law hat-trick seemed to have seen off Sporting Lisbon.

Law maintained his remarkable scoring run and United's momentum by scoring the ubiquitous hat-trick to settle a marathon FA Cup tie with Sunderland and put the Cup holders through to the semi-final.

Despite Law's sensational form, March proved to be a cruel month, as inside of four days United were ejected from both Cup competitions. In a mud bath at Hillsborough, West Ham knocked the Reds out of the FA Cup, despite another goal from Law. Then, in a horror show in Lisbon, Sporting overturned a three-goal deficit to knock United out of Europe. With a backlog of league games building up, a series of disappointing draws, culminating in a defeat to Champions-elect, Liverpool, in early April spelt all but the end of United's title hopes. By the time the Trautman testimonial came about, United's search for honours looked to be over, but they still had important games to play as they sought to tie down the runners-up spot and guarantee further European football. So, it was probably with very mixed feelings that the City fans looked down on their former player, back in a sky-blue shirt, but now undisputedly the 'King' of Old Trafford. Already on forty-four goals for the season, he would finish in a couple of weeks with a tally of forty-six goals from just forty-one appearances in all competitions.

Bobby Charlton, the other 'red' in 'blue', was always my favourite player, from the first moment I saw him play in this eventful season, right through to the modern day. That's quite a statement when you think of the wealth of talent that have played for United from the sixties until the present day.

I had first spotted him on the inside cover of that old football annual that had the grim pictures of the grounded aircraft. He featured in one of those famous artist impressions of the football action that illuminated the page with their bold bright colours. In this illustration from the Cup Final, Bobby, who seemed to have a lot more hair than he had by nineteen sixty-four, was captured in a typically graceful pose about to strike the ball as Bolton's Tommy Banks slid in to tackle. The picture caption had told me that Bobby had been a 'big threat' to Bolton, and indeed he had come the closest to a United goal when his shot cannoned off the post. Bobby had a miraculous escape from the plane and, with the help of Harry Gregg, had escaped with his life. Here he was, just three months later, trying to win the Cup for United!

Between the horrors of the crash and this testimonial picture Bobby maintained his position as a regular England international, and an ever-present as Busby tried to rebuild after Munich. In fact, in the season directly after Munich, Bobby, as a sharpshooting left winger (or outside left as they were called) was the teams' top scorer with twenty-nine goals as the Reds defied expectations by finishing League runners-up.

United had struggled to maintain that form in subsequent seasons, but Bobby maintained his reputation as a dashing forward with a cannon ball shot, claiming over twenty goals a season for two more seasons. Although the goal tally dropped in the early sixties, Bobby remained a crucial player for Busby as he toiled to rebuild the side.

However, by the '63-64 season, with United enjoying their best season since the crash, Bobby's position in the team began to change. In his previous role, Bobby was seen as the flying winger, popularly known as the whiz bang kid, as the goals flowed. By the middle of this season, Busby had decided that Bobby would be more effective for the team at inside left, or in today's parlance, the central midfield. Busby felt that the mature Charlton could contribute more from this position but had also earmarked his winger position for a genius he had in the youth side called George Best. Bobby still retained his trademark shooting from long distances, with spectacular goals, but married this with a graceful range of long passing that opened up opportunities for others.

Although the spectacular goals were an obvious focus for a young and impressionable fan, Bobby Charlton offered more than this. Bobby seemed to be built on heroic lines, the survivor from Munich, whose honest toil in a red shirt was only matched by his fair sense of play; he was Hollywood's Gary Cooper incarnate. Bobby, to my eyes epitomised a graceful dignity in the way he played. He was the ultimate good guy and I was so proud he represented my team. Making our way to the testimonial game on the bus, I was rather hoping that Bobby would mark my attendance with one of his spectacular long-range goals for Trautman's testimonial. Bobby rated the goalkeeper very highly. In another of my football annuals, the 1960 copy of, 'Bobby Charlton's book of soccer', Bobby had named his present World eleven and the German keeper was in it. Given that United's Harry Gregg had been named the goalkeeper of the 1958 World Cup tournament and the Russian keeper, Lev Yashin, was in his prime, this was praise indeed.

Even though Denis and Bobby were star turns in United's great season and I had by this time been to a couple of matches at Old Trafford, the game I remember most clearly from 'my' first season was the Bert Trautman testimonial game. The match was big news in Manchester and had been all over the Manchester Evening News for weeks in advance. Both Manchester clubs were promoting it and it was even possible to buy tickets for it at Old Trafford in advance of the game. The press reported that John Willet, of the United supporter's association, was selling tickets for the game outside Old Trafford, during their Easter fixtures. The larger-than-life City goalkeeper transcended any club rivalry, and it would seem that all sorts of publicity was used by the United club to drum up sales for the testimonial game. There was a testimonial concert at the United supporter's association at Collyhurst, at which Bert and the reigning Miss Great Britain attended. The Cromford club, the inner sanctum of Matt Busby and his entourage, announced that they would hold a dinner dance, with Bert as the guest of honour.

Maybe the most surprising aspect of the game was that United appeared to be content to move a fixture to accommodate the testimonial. Given that the match was during the season, and when it was being planned United were fighting for trophies on three fronts, this was quite remarkable. Initially, the fixture list showed that United would entertain Sheffield United on Saturday the eleventh of April. Nearer the time of that date, it became apparent that United would have to move the game because England had a fixture that weekend. The usual place for any re-arranged games was the following midweek, so Wednesday the fifteenth of April seemed to be the likely date, until it was realised that this was the date earmarked for the Trautman testimonial. United solved the potential problem by agreeing to play Sheffield United on the Monday evening of April the thirteenth, and thus allowing the testimonial game to go ahead in the scheduled slot of April fifteenth. Bert Trautman was suitably grateful, commenting: 'Matt Busby has been great over this, in addition to steering clear of my match date, he has already provided five of his best players', adding, 'who else would have done that in the face of all the demands that could be on him by that time'. Matt Busby had given his wholehearted endorsement for the match, even using his manager's column in the United programme for the Easter Monday game against Fulham. Busby declared himself 'delighted to help' in forming a joint Manchester eleven. Bert, he added was 'always worth watching as a brilliant, graceful goalkeeper in his heyday with a remarkable, almost effortless style'. So it was that United's Noel Cantwell, Bill Foulkes and Maurice Setters joined Denis and Bobby to form half of the Manchester team that would play in front of Trautman.

Bert Trautman had been on quite a journey. It was some fifteen years before this that the Maine Road club had controversially signed a former German paratrooper and prisoner of war, just four years after the cessation of hostilities. Signing the giant keeper from St. Helens Town had caused some adverse headlines, and many of the City support were reported to have not renewed season tickets in protest. Despite such an uncertain start to his career, Trautman had quickly won the City fans over with a series of brave and brilliant saves as he made the goalkeepers shirt his own. Throughout the nineteen fifties he was City's brilliant last line of defence, and helped them win silverware when he was memorably part of the 1956 FA Cup winning side, despite playing with a broken neck. However, the late fifties and early sixties saw a marked decline in the Maine Road club's fortunes, and it was a widely held view that only Trautman's brilliance had kept City in the top league year after year. That battle, however, had been lost the previous season, when the 'Law' penalty had seen the blues relegated. Although by that time the veteran keeper was not first choice for the club and subsequently had decided to retire this very season.

The 'International eleven' that made up the opposition were almost equally the main attraction of the game. Looking back on their line up now, the term 'International' seems to have been a very loose definition of the term. I considered that surely with a title like that I might have seen the cream of European football (especially as European competition was well established by then), or more particularly given Trautman's nationality, a German star, but no, the team was made up of ten Englishmen and a Scot! They were nearly all players with northern clubs, with the furthest travelled coming from Stoke! They were, however, all internationals with some of the famous names of English soccer playing. The most fuss was made of the famous Stanley Mathews and Tom Finney combination. Finney, had retired four years earlier, but Mathews at the age of forty-eight was still playing. In-fact, Mathews had helped Stoke City to promotion the previous season. Unfortunately, when we got to the game we found out that Finney wasn't playing, nor another big name, Don Revie. Although Finney's absence seemed to have given me another United player, as Albert Quixall was named as his replacement.

THE MATCH: MANCHESTER XI v INTERNATIONAL XI   15/4/1964

It was a pleasant warm evening as myself and my sister got off the bus and made our way to the Maine Road ground. The game had clearly caught the Manchester public's imagination, as a large crowd was making its way in the same direction. It was, apparently, a lot more people than the turnstiles were used to dealing with and large queues snaked back from the turnstile gates. Later, an attendance of forty-seven thousand was officially recorded, although many found unofficial ways of entering the ground and a figure of sixty thousand might have been more accurate. Over half a century later it is a hazy memory of the game, but certain things seem to have lingered. The teams came out to quite a fanfare. I could just about make out the giant figure of Trautman leading out the Manchester team and the 'international' eleven seemed to be in some sort of striped outfit. If truth be told, I saw little of the action; as a small nine-year-old in a mass of swaying people I could make out very little. Eventually, later in the game my vantage point did improve due to the generosity of some of the crowd nearby. In a moment akin to something you might see in one of those old black and white Ealing films, a nearby chap reckoned the 'nipper' couldn't see much and persuaded my sister to allow me to be passed forward, so that eventually I landed right by the edge of the pitch and pretty close to the corner flag.

Almost immediately in my first clear sight of the action, Stanley Mathews trotted over to take a corner kick. He was greeted by warm applause and I had a close-up view of one of the greats of English soccer as he carefully took the kick that arced into the penalty area, where Trautman eventually claimed it. In retrospect, this is the strange thing; I have such a clear memory of Mathews, but saw very little of my two United heroes, although both scored in the game, with Law typically scoring twice. I only knew this because I read it in the paper the next day.

The game itself, as is often the case with these testimonials, didn't seem to be a particularly serious encounter, and the first goal seemed to typify this. Setters, United's hard man of the time, booting the ball high into the air, over his goalkeeper Trautman's head and into his own net. Although I couldn't quite see this, I was confused by the fact that he was supposed to be kicking the other way! But from the amused response of the players I gathered that maybe the game wasn't that important. Nonetheless, Setters didn't seem to be cowed by the experience, and in the next day's papers joked that he had always wanted to score a goal past Bert

Trautman. The game finished five-four to the Manchester team, but myself and my sister were making our way home when the referee blew the final whistle a couple of minutes early due to a crowd invasion of the pitch.

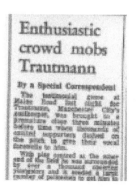

TEAM LINE-UP

Manchester XI: Trautman, Leivers, Cantwell, Setters, Foulkes, Oakes, Murray, Kevan, Charlton, Law, Wagstaffe

International XI: Springett (Shef. Wed), Armfield (Blackpool), Wilson (Huddersfield) Clayton (Blackburn), Adamson (Burnley), Miller (Burnley), Mathews (Stoke), Douglas (Blackburn), Quixall (Man.U), Johnstone (Oldham), Connelly (Man. U)

⚽⚽⚽

So began over fifty years supporting United with the strange memory of two of their greatest ever players running around the pitch in City shirts!

Bobby Charlton remains, for many people, United's greatest ever player. His 758 club appearances was a club record for thirty-five years until Ryan Giggs surpassed this total in 2008. Scoring 249 goals for the Reds, he won every medal the game had to offer, winning League Championship medals, an FA Cup winners' medal and of course a European Cup winners' medal. In addition to this he was capped by England 106 times, scoring 49 goals for his Country. Bobby is one of that exclusive group of English players to have won a World Cup winners' medal, this together with his club honours makes him a truly unique individual. Harold Riley's painting of the United maestro summed him up perfectly. The inscription read: 'A man of quiet and dignified presence, who has showed undying loyalty to United'.

Denis Law almost certainly enjoyed the best years of his career at United. Despite suffering from injuries that impacted on his appearances in his later years at the club, he still accumulated 404 games for United and his 237 goals leaves him the third highest goal scorer in the club's illustrious history. Given that he was sharing a forward line with fellow European footballers of the year, Charlton and Best, and yet the striker was known as the 'King', tells us all we need to know about how important Denis was to United when he was in his imperious pomp.

THE BIGGER PICTURE

Matt Busby became manager of United immediately after the Second World War. He was effectively the first modern tracksuit manager. While he was without a home ground for his first three seasons, he did inherit the nucleus of a good side. Already at the club were the likes of Carey, Morris, Mitten, Rowley and Pearson. Busby had benefited by the provident approach of the club when they had set up the MUJACs (Manchester United Junior Athletic Club) in 1938, quite a few of these players had graduated from this source, so Busby was able to limit his transfer activity to just one significant player, Jimmy Delaney. Busby quickly showed some subtle positional changes and almost immediately imbued the team with a creative attacking philosophy that would become the trademark of all his successful sides. Busby's United were soon established as one of the league's top sides, with four runner-up positions in his first five seasons before winning the title in his sixth season. It was the clubs first title since 1911, and together with their exciting victory in the FA Cup Final of 1948, Busby and United had become an established force in the game.

As Busby's first great side began to age, the manager showed a revolutionary farsightedness to gradually introduce a set of young players from his youth team. Between 1952 and 1955, Busby transformed the side with players promoted from the youth team; the 'Busby Babes' were born. With the addition of Tommy Taylor, purchased from Barnsley, the Babes were the talk of football, and large crowds flocked to see them play. By 1956 United had returned to the pinnacle of English football, winning the league by a whopping eleven points, at a time of two points for a win. Winning the title once again the following season, Busby's United were desperately close to achieving the first 'double' (winning the FA Cup and the League) of the century, only to lose the Cup Final to Aston Villa in unfortunate circumstances, losing their goalkeeper in the process.

In addition to establishing his team at the top of the English game, the visionary Busby went against Football League advice and entered United in the relatively new

European Cup. So by that 1956-57 season for the first time an English club were fighting to win trophies on three fronts. United thrilled their supporters with some remarkable victories on these new European nights, only going out at the semi-final stage to a powerful Real Madrid team. There was a general feeling that with this experience United could go one better the following season, and their brilliant young side were making exciting progress in all competitions, but then came Munich.

MANAGERIAL RECORD OF MATT BUSBY 1946 – 1958

	League	FA Cup	Europe
1946-47	2nd	Round 4	
1947-48	2nd	**WON**	
1948-49	2nd	SF	
1949-50	4th	Round 6	
1950-51	2nd	Round 6	
1951-52	**WON**	Round 3	
1952-53	8th	Round 5	
1953-54	4th	Round 3	
1954-55	5th	Round 4	
1955-56	**WON**	Round 3	
1956-57	**WON**	Finalist	EC SF
1957-58*	9th	Finalist	EC SF

Matches played: 554 (Wins: 52.5% *League and Cup matches after 5/2/58 not counted, Jimmy Murphy took over as care-taker manager for the rest of that season)

Most expensive signing: Tommy Taylor (£29,999)

Most significant youth player debuts: John Aston (senior), Shay Brennan, Roger Byrne, Bobby Charlton, Eddie Colman, Jack Crompton, Duncan Edwards, Bill Foulkes, Mark Jones, Wilf McGuinness, Charlie Mitten, John Morris, Stan Pearson, David Pegg

Not surprisingly, it took Matt Busby and Manchester United some time to recover from the horrors of Munich. The crash virtually obliterated the whole of the young 'Busby Babes' side which had looked destined to dominate English football for many years to come. Despite the heroics of reaching the 1958 Cup final and the incredible achievement of finishing league runners up in the first season after Munich, the years between the crash and 1964 had been years of struggle. Remarkably, the club were still able to count on some good home-produced players, including, of course, Bobby Charlton, but unsurprisingly Busby had to bring out the cheque book in order to fill some of the gaps. Despite this, the club began to drift down the table, and there were even rumours that Busby, so clearly effected both physically and psychologically by Munich, might give up management. Four years after Munich, United were down to fifteenth in the league, a position unheard of throughout his tenure at the club. Worse was to follow, as despite purchasing Denis Law for the record fee, United were embroiled in a desperate relegation struggle in '62-63, only escaping the drop by a few points. However, United's glorious victory in the 1963 FA Cup Final proved to be a turning point for Busby and United. It was not only United's first trophy since Munich, it would also act as a springboard for the exciting '63-64 season.

MANAGERIAL RECORD OF MATT BUSBY 1958 – 1964

	League	League Cup	FA Cup	Europe
1958-59	2nd		Round 3	
1959-60	7th		Round 5	
1960-61	7th	Round 2	Round 4	
1961-62	15th		SF	
1962-63	19th		**WON**	
1963-64	2nd		SF	ECWC QF

Matches played: 289 (Wins: 46%)

Most expensive signing: Denis Law (£115,000)

Most significant youth player debuts: George Best, David Sadler, Nobby Stiles

3

IN THE PICTURE

GEORGE BEST

I love this picture of the immortal George Best. It is not the more famous 'el Beatle' picture, taken two years later, but one taken in the local park in March 1964. However, I much prefer this picture because in many ways it's the essence of George; just as he was 'discovered'. 'Remember me for my football', was George's epitaph, and this picture encapsulates the pure joy George derived from playing the beautiful game.

George is enjoying a kickabout in the local park; it looks like Chorlton park, just down the road from where I lived and close to his landlady, Mrs Fullaway's lodgings. The picture was taken just a couple of weeks before I saw Bobby and Denis in the testimonial match. The photograph was to mark the Belfast boy's arrival on the big stage; the night before it was taken, George had scored a dramatic late equaliser in the game of the season, an FA Cup tie with Sunderland. He had only been playing in the first team proper for three months, and this game culminated a remarkable run of eleven games for the Reds. It was a set of matches that had helped turn United's season around and announced to the wider football world that an amazing new talent had arrived.

It's an amazing photoshoot really. Could anyone imagine today's overpaid and overrated stars, going into a park with a group of lads for a game of centring and heading. Yet it was not that unusual for George to get one of those plastic footballs you could buy at the local shop and go for a kickaround. In Duncan Hamilton's biography of Best, he quotes Mrs Fullaway's son, describing how George 'loved' to find a patch of land for a kickaround and how, 'the neighbourhood joined in. We'd soon have an eleven a side going'. In many ways it was typical of an age before computers and mobile phones and I had plenty of practice myself, trying to save my brother's headers! In fact, I could have been the goalkeeper in the photograph; I certainly had that jumper!

The Football Pink was my main source of information regarding George's dramatic emergence that season. He had made his actual debut, as all United fans know, by 'twisting the blood' of West Brom full-back, Williams, in a United victory in September 1963. However, nothing was then seen of him and he was certainly off my radar, as Denis the King hogged the headlines with his scoring feats. Given that when he made his debut, he cut a slight waif-like figure, there may have been some doubts about his physical durability, although it would appear, at least initially, that the canny Busby was merely holding him back. Jimmy Murphy, Busby's right-hand man, who had kept the flag flying after Munich, was in no doubt that Best was a unique and special talent. Duncan Hamilton, in his biography of Best, commented that Murphy applied a light touch when it came to the training of Best, that regimental drills were eschewed, as Murphy, 'wanted Best to remain as he'd originally seen him – daring and full of tricks'.

Nonetheless, to the general public George had disappeared, learning in the youth side no doubt. It was therefore something of a surprise when his name suddenly appeared on the team sheet for the home game with Burnley three days after Christmas. United had endured a dreadful festive set of games, with Everton thrashing them four-nil and then on boxing day Burnley increased the torment with a six-one hiding. The alarm bells were ringing for Matt Busby as United's most promising season since Munich seemed to be in danger of imploding. Things were not helped by talisman Denis Law's ongoing suspension. The local Manchester Guardian newspaper wondered what nostrums the manager might come up with. Busby responded with the introduction of two out-and-out wingers in Anderson and Best. The programme notes indicated that both wingers had shown up well in a youth tie at Barrow, but facing the experienced Burnley full-backs of Angus and Elder was surely a different proposition. Anderson impressed with his skill that day, but subsequently had to settle for a career in the lower leagues. For George Best, though, this was the start of a permanent role in the side and over the next dozen games it was to have a galvanising effect on United's season. Burnley were thrashed five-one, and George showed there was more to his game than dribbling by scoring the third goal with a cool finish. The Observer newspaper the next day was in no doubt that United had uncovered a gem, commenting: 'he is a slight, dark, casual Irishman with lovely ball control'. They would however add a caveat that would be repeated in the months and years ahead, that he 'has a lot to learn when not to shoot'. This kind of comment was often used about a young Ronaldo nearly forty years later. Genius, it seems, is not always recognised at first sight.

So, with the dawn of 1964, George became a regular first team player, and within seven days he was partly responsible for United's sterling comeback, away to Southampton in the FA Cup. United, the Cup holders, were facing an embarrassing elimination at the Dell, as the home side led two-nil at half-time. Again, Best's wing play helped to transform the game, and with United scoring three times, the Reds progressed in the most exciting manner. Despite being part of the eleven that suffered a surprise defeat in the league to Birmingham, Busby didn't 'rest' his newfound talent, and George kept his place for the next league fixture, a match that would go down in

United's history as a watershed moment. The four-one rout of West Brom at the Hawthorns was more than a much-needed league victory against tough opponents, it was the first United line up to feature the special trinity of Charlton, Law, and Best.

As if to emphasise the significance of that match played on the eighteenth of January, all three players scored. Charlton freed from the straitjacket of being out on the wing, powered a shot home from central midfield, Law naturally scored twice and Best running England full-back, Howe, ragged virtually dribbled the ball into the net. A template was struck that day, which would serve the club so well over the next four years.

United maintained their FA Cup run, and this time George was part of the supporting cast as Denis scored yet another hat-trick as Bristol Rovers were thrashed at Old Trafford. By the start of February, United's title hopes were reignited, as Best was part of a settled forward line that saw off a fancied Arsenal side at Old Trafford. United's league inconsistency caught up with them in a narrow defeat at Leicester, although the Belfast boy thought he had saved them with a late goal; unfortunately ruled out for offside. George's form was revelatory, and Busby resisted the natural caution of resting his new star in the Cup by selecting Best for a tough-looking fifth round tie at Barnsley. Despite the predictably tough tackling methods of the Barnsley defenders, Best was sublime, scoring with a smart shot on twenty-five minutes and then took the breath away with a mazy dribble that took him around the goalkeeper before squaring the ball for Law to slot into the empty net. The following Wednesday, the irrepressible Best was at it again, and this time it was the notoriously hard Bolton defence that were shredded as George inspired a crushing win that had echoes of the babes' seven-two victory in the season of Munich. Hartle, the uncompromising Bolton right-back was, according to the Manchester Guardian, 'bewildered' by the winger as George dribbled past him and put United in front after just three minutes. Hartle reverted to more traditional methods later in the half, as the Guardian reported the Irishman was 'heavily brought down, needing prolonged treatment' to gain United a penalty, which Law missed. In the second half George wriggled past some statuesque defenders to add the third in United's five-nil win.

United's new discovery was now grabbing the headlines, as copy writers delighted in the use of his surname to paraphrase United's accent. The next league game, away at Blackburn days later was considered to be 'The Best yet', as United recorded another comfortable win over close rivals that put United within a couple of points of the top spot. George had, in no time, established himself as a vital part of the most attractive forward line in the country, and yet another capacity away crowd illustrated the growing appeal of this exciting United side. The press reports had almost become conventional: 'Experienced Blackburn full-back Bray run ragged as Best is instrumental in United's victory'.

Since Matt Busby's far-sighted decision to enter European competition in the mid-fifties, United were, as then, and would be so many times in the years ahead, fighting glorious campaigns on three fronts. The European Cup Winners Cup competition gave the season a colourful continental flavour, although it was the outstanding Spurs side (first winners of a European trophy and existing holders) that United had knocked out to reach the quarter finals. In this round they were due to play Portuguese side, Sporting Lisbon, with the first leg due at Old Trafford on the twenty sixth of February, just four days after the Blackburn game. Once more, Busby resisted any urge to rest Best, as he was picked to make his European debut against the skilful Portuguese. Once more, the frenzied atmosphere of the maximum Old Trafford crowd didn't faze the young Irishman as he fitted into a forward line that saw Law score the, almost obligatory, hat-trick in what seemed to be a decisive four-one win.

THE MATCH: UNITED 3 SUNDERLAND 3   29/2/1964

In terms of priorities, though, the FA Cup was considered the second most important trophy of the three United were competing for. Indeed, for some, the Cup, with its televised national coverage of Cup Final day, was the most important. Best had been instrumental in United's FA Cup run that had gained momentum by the end of February, and the Reds were drawn at home to play an upwardly mobile Sunderland team. The famous north-east side were enjoying a marvellous season, destined to fight off Leeds for the second division title. They had predictably brought thousands of fans to Old Trafford, and they fancied their chances. Although, in essence, their strength lay in their teamwork, their outstanding players were their athletic young goalkeeper, Montgomery, the skilful midfield schemer, Crossan, and the lion-hearted club legend, Charlie Hurley. With nine victories in this Best spell of eleven games, United were warm favourites, and the seasons highest crowd of over sixty-three thousand were in attendance. However, it was Sunderland that started the better, taking a grip on the game that United were unable to counter. Instead of United's characteristic fluid inter-passing, their play was beset by misplaced passes and wild shooting. Instead it was Sunderland, roared on by their passionate supporters, that took a deserved one-nil half-time lead. Eric Todd, doyen of northern reporters, wrote in the Manchester Guardian that only Best 'varied his tactics, realising that orthodoxy was a waste of time', and lamented that Charlton and Law were having 'an off day'. Things didn't get any better early in the second half when the clever, Crossan, escaped down the left wing and then cut in to fire past Gaskell. United did pull a goal back fortuitously when Hurley put through his own goal, but when Crossan was upended and then rifled in the subsequent penalty, United were heading out of the Cup. There were less than five minutes left when United finally roused themselves and put the Sunderland goal under sustained pressure. In a scenario that would become so common over the years, United rallied chasing a lost cause and, against all probability, redeemed themselves with two goals in the dying minutes. It was George Best who was central to United's resurrection. Firstly, his perfectly in-swinging corner was headed into the net by Charlton, and then with two minutes left he typically moved in from the wing to find a crucial bit of space in the penalty box to stab in the equaliser. In the Sunday Observer, the great Hugh McIlvanney was in no doubt he had seen the birth of a star. 'His shot', he said, 'was comparatively gentle but it gained in menace by going through half a dozen legs'. It sparked tumultuous celebrations on the terraces. McIlvanney talked about a 'primitive roar', that announced the arrival of a special talent.

It was this relatively unspectacular goal that truly marked the arrival of George Best, leading to that photograph in the papers and his domination of the headlines that would become so commonplace in the years to come. Inside of two months, the unknown boy from Belfast, with just one game last September, was the toast of the town and now the papers couldn't get enough of his story. Suddenly, instead of the text being about the details of the match, the Monday papers were focusing on the person behind the player. George was quoted as claiming his mother would be, 'pleased as punch', and the papers reported that his father and grandfather had flown in from Belfast for the match. George commented: 'My mother sent a letter with my father saying she hoped I had a good game and would score. She'll be tickled pink now – she's just about my biggest fan'. Finally, they returned to the game and George described that goal: 'I thought we'd had it, then suddenly I was in front of the goal with the ball at my feet, so I just slammed it as hard as I could, I still can't believe I scored.' There was to be no after match celebrations, claimed the paper, as the Beatle-cut seventeen-year-old dashed home to watch the Beatles on tv.

Sunderland foiled at very last

Crossan teaches Law a lesson

By ERIC TODD : Manchester United 3, Sunderland 3

Manchester United, seemingly on their death-bed, tore themselves from the undertaker's grasp and drew 3-3 with Sunderland in their FA Challenge Cup sixth-round game. After such a reprieve, United probably will win Wednesday's replay at Roker Park.

Dame Fortune and Lady Luck, those seductive and much sought-after guests, were an unconscionable long time over accepting United's invitation to Old Trafford on Saturday. They looked in for a minute early in the second half, decided they did not like the look of Hurley, departed, and did not return until the party was breaking up. They smiled on Charlton, drooled over young Best, and that was it. Women !

do to the leaders of the Second Division. They soon learned different. They learned further that if Law and Charlton have an off day for one reason or another, the rest of the players are expected to make up the deficiencies. On Saturday, they failed miserably to do so. Only Best of the forwards tried to vary his tactics, only Best realised that orthodoxy was a waste of time. In defence, Foulkes was harassed by the diminutive Sharkey but he played a grand game and without him and Dunne, one of the most improved backs in the land, United would have floundered. It is hard to believe they will pick the same team and make the same mistakes on Wednesday.

There was more reconnaissance than shooting in the first stages during which Law and Hurley fouled each other for the only

✜✜✜

A UNITED TEAM IN TIME

FA Cup Round 6 Line-up; Gaskell, Brennan, Dunne, Crerand, Foulkes, Setters, Herd, Stiles, Charlton, Law, Best

The dramatic finish had forced a replay at Sunderland's Roker Park the following Wednesday. The games were now becoming part of serial, that so characterised the glamour of the FA Cup and attracted the wider public. Interest in United's late deliverance was reaching epic proportions, and thousands (including, mystifyingly to me, my brother) now descended on Roker for the nighttime game. In those far-off days, virtually all games were pay at the turnstiles non-ticket affairs, and this replay became a notorious fixture in the dangerous levels of overcrowding that occurred. A capacity of forty-six thousand people was quickly reached, but the thousands milling around outside forced their entry, kicking down fencing to gain admittance. Folklore has it that seventy thousand people witnessed, with a sense of déjà vu, a repeat of the first game. Once more, Sunderland were the better team, leading twice, but twice United fought back with late equalisers; the second being seconds from the end of extra time. Eric Todd once again praised Best as 'United's outstanding forward', but reckoned that United had 'unbelievably escaped' to a third replay at Huddersfield. After the Roker fiasco, this was now an all ticket game, and finally United showed their true colours by coming from one down to score five, with Law contributing a hat-trick. The three matches had been watched by an official attendance of 165,379, but in reality, by many more. It's incredible to state today, that the FA Cup was so important, that United's second leg tie with Sporting Lisbon due to be played on the date of the first replay was postponed, so that the FA Cup tie could go ahead. United and George, in what seemed to be a fairy tale two months, were one match from the big Final at Wembley and well placed in both the League and European competitions.

However, it was not to be for George and United. Just five days after the Sunderland victory United lost the semi-final to West Ham in a mud bath at Hillsborough. Then four days after that reversal, United incredibly lost their European second leg in Lisbon, thumped five-nil. All the cup games had caused a league backlog, and after a series of wasteful draws, defeat at Anfield to the eventual champions meant that United had to settle for the runners-up spot. Despite the disappointing nature of these events, there was no mistaking that this was United's best post-Munich season, and in **George Best** they had uncovered one of, if not their greatest ever player. Over the next four seasons United and Best would win the League Championship twice, and Best would score the crucial second goal as United finally won the European Cup, ten years after Munich, when they defeated Benfica four-one.

THE BIGGER PICTURE

Following the near misses of the previous season, United reclaimed the first division title in '64-65. It had taken seven years to build a side to replace the Babes, and with three of the world's greatest players allied to club stalwarts Dunne, Crerand and Stiles, it was fair to say that Busby had developed a side that stood in fair comparison.

Only a country's champions could enter the European Cup, and so this title triumph opened the doors on Europe's premier competition for the first time since Munich. United's superlative form in the competition had them amongst the favourites, and this was reinforced by a breathtaking five-one victory over Benfica in the quarter finals. Benfica were one of the established forces in European football, boasting one of the world's greatest players, Eusebio, they hadn't been beaten at home in nine years. Therefore, the pundits did not favour United, who only gained a slender one goal advantage from the first leg. However, in one of the club's greatest ever performances, a superlative display of attacking football overwhelmed Benfica; it was arguably George Best's finest moment, as his two goals and an assist in the opening sixteen minutes decided the game. There was therefore massive disappointment when United succumbed to a semi-final defeat to Partisan Belgrade. With United unable to win the league the following season, there was a general feeling that Busby might have missed his last chance in his crusade to win the European Cup. However, United won the league once more in '66-67, typically clinching the title with a stunning six-one defeat of West Ham, and this once more allowed them to compete in the European Cup. This time United went all the way, beating Real Madrid with a typically audacious late flourish in the semi-finals, and then beating Benfica four-one in a memorable Final at Wembley. Busby's mission seemed complete. The man who had brought European football to English clubs now managed the country's first winner of the prestigious trophy; it was exactly ten years after he had lost virtually his whole team at Munich.

Sir Matt Busby, as he then became, announced his retirement the following January, and the '68-69 season was his twenty-fourth, and last, with the club. Eamon Dunphy, in his seminal biography of Busby, "A Strange Kind of Glory", summed him up adroitly, when he called him 'the last great football man'.

MANAGERIAL RECORD OF MATT BUSBY (1964-69)

	League	League Cup	FA Cup	Europe
1964-65	**WON**		SF	ICFC / SF
1965-66	4th		SF	EC / SF
1966-67	**WON**	Round 2	Round 4	
1967-68	2nd		Round 3	**EC / WON**
1968-69	11th		QF	EC / SF

Matches played: 275 (Wins: 52%)

Most expensive signing: Willie Morgan (£105,000)

Most significant youth player debuts: John Aston (Junior), John Fitzpatrick, Brian Kidd, Bobby Noble

4

IN THE PICTURE

GEORGE BEST & WILF McGUINNESS

Here is a very different picture of George, taken five years after that happy snap in the park. It is a photograph taken on the third of December 1969, of the players leaving the pitch at the end of the first leg of a League Cup semi-final, played at Maine Road against United's local rivals, City. An animated George Best looks angrily at referee Jack Taylor and has to be separated from him from the adidas bag-laden trainer, Jack Crompton. United's new manager, Wilf McGuiness, looked equally dismayed and looks stonily ahead. The referee, Jack Taylor - later to earn some tabloid fame for being England's representative in the 1974 World Cup Final - seems to be saying something as he strides from the pitch. It is possibly the expression on the face of the local constabulary that tells us the most, as we have just witnessed an explosive and controversial moment that would have big implications for both George and United. Just two minutes from the end of a hard-fought and close match on City's quagmire-like pitch, Taylor had controversially awarded a penalty to City, which when Francis Lee converted gave the home side a 2-1 victory in the tie. Best, who had cut a frustrated figure throughout the match, felt like he had not had many decisions in his favour and, obviously incensed by the penalty decision, confronted Taylor as they left the pitch and knocked the ball out of the referee's hands. The picture shows the aftermath of the incident, as Crompton shepherds Best off the pitch.

Much has changed for George since the Sunderland game. In that time he has become a vital player for the Reds and in just five years he has picked up two Championship medals and a European Cup winning medal. He is now one of the greatest players in the world and at the age of twenty-two in 1968 he was named European footballer of the year. That award was less than twelve months ago, but this is now a different story, as George is the main man of a United side struggling in the immediate aftermath of Sir Matt Busby's retirement. In some ways this picture encapsulates those changes, particularly for the two men featured in the photograph. George, at the age of just twenty-three, a multiple winner and now United's most important player but playing in a struggling and declining team, is perhaps weighed down with the responsibilities that his fame has brought. Certainly, the carefree smile of the Belfast boy is missing on this dark night at Maine Road. Instead, are we seeing some of the demons that would blight his career from this point onwards? For Wilf, 'Busby babe' and man, plucked from the shadows just eight months before to become manager of one of the world's most famous clubs, the future looks equally troubled. Under enormous pressure to succeed and struggling to justify his appointment, this match represents his one big chance to establish himself and win the time to build up his own managerial career. Just ninety minutes from Wembley, if United can win this semi-final, then they would have a winnable Final against West Brom to come and a potential first trophy that would stabilise his reign.

These were puzzling times for this teenage fan of United, as I watched the Reds lose in such cruel fashion, one was not downcast, we had the second leg to come at home after all, and surely all would be well. It was hardly a time of crisis, hadn't we been just one dodgy refereeing decision away from a crack at another European Cup Final just seven months before. The papers had shown a photograph of Denis Law's shot, well over the line, but we weren't given the goal and it was AC Milan that made the 1969 Final. Nonetheless, times were changing. The old certainties and swagger were disappearing, and for this United supporter more uncertain times lay ahead. Most of these uncertainties had their roots in what seemed to be the sudden decision of Sir Matt Busby to announce his retirement in the January of 1969. Although this wouldn't take effect until the summer, this was major news that made front page headlines. In some ways it was yet another story about Britain's most famous and well covered football club, but in other more profound ways it was to be a watershed for United's supporters and the fortunes of the club in the years ahead.

Many had thought that Sir Matt, as he became after winning the European Cup in '68, might have chosen that date to retire. It could have seemed a natural moment to make the break, having achieved his crusade to bring that trophy back for United exactly ten years after the crash. To my teenage eyes, Busby seemed an old man and certainly the crash had left its scars, both physically and psychologically, but he was still two years shy of his sixtieth birthday. Instead, he continued at the helm, leading United into the next season, but by January 6, 1969, I was reading the shock news that he would retire at the end of the season.

The announcement was dominating the news on both the front and back pages. It might have been a major news story, but to United fans it was more important than that; Matt Busby, it seemed to me, *was* Manchester United. The journalist, Frank McGee, unaware of the later building of the Busby statue, said that they would never need to erect a monument to him, as 'he had built one himself at Old Trafford, from the cellars upwards, literally'. He had been the boss at Old Trafford for all of my life and for many years before that; twenty-three years since taking up the post at the end of the Second World War. Reading through detail of the story it soon became apparent that the board seemed to be in as much shock as everybody else, as they talked about 'reluctantly' accepting his decision, but adding the important caveat that Busby would take up the position of general manager from the summer onwards. To my juvenile mind there seemed a certain comfort in this. Sir Matt, who's very life's work had been the club, would not be cast aside. How comforting it was to think that he would still be available to offer wise council, no doubt. An older, more experienced person might have looked at the Manchester Evening news photo montage of available managerial talent and deduced that experienced, independent managers might not have been so enamoured of his new position.

It didn't inhibit the bookies, who immediately installed the highest profile manager in the game as short priced favourite. Don Revie was manager of reigning League Champions, Leeds, and the papers were full of stories linking him to the job. I wasn't particularly happy about this; Leeds football philosophy seemed the polar opposite of football 'played by Matt Busby'. I needn't have worried, as the very next day Revie ruled himself out of the job, commenting he was happy at Leeds. Matt Busby had outlined that United were now after a 'tracksuit' manager, and he even stipulated an age group; 'early thirties and not over forty-five'. However, tellingly he added that they also wanted an experienced man as United were 'not in a position to experiment'. Of the young managers, Brian Clough seemed to meet the criteria, having just gained promotion with Derby County, but his abrasive style was not likely to go down well with the powers that be at United. The next day's Manchester Guardian story by Eric Todd proved to be much more perceptive, under a headline that read 'Manchester United could keep job in the family'. Jimmy Murphy, Jack Crompton and John Aston seemed to be ruled out on age grounds, and that didn't leave many other options. The reserve team coach, Wilf McGuinness, seemed to be where the paper was pointing. The bookies didn't agree, and Wilf was still available at long odds. Instead, they looked at the identikit and increasingly came up with the name of Noel Cantwell. The old United skipper, who had lifted the FA Cup in 1963, was fourteen months into his managerial career at Coventry City, and in terms of youth, experience and links to Busby, this seemed a persuasive argument. In those far-off days, there was no rolling Sky Sports football news and so it became perfectly normal for the papers to drop the story after a few days and nothing more was heard about the job. It was nearly four months later, on April ninth, that United made the official announcement that they had appointed Wilf McGuinness to the vacant post. Strangely, on that day Cantwell's side beat United two-one. I studied the photographs of the press conference. McGuinness, flanked by Sir Matt, smiled at the camera; the local lad from Collyhurst had done well, he was just thirty-one years of age. I noted in the Guardian report that Wilf's official title was 'coach', and pondered over the last sentence that said: 'He will take up his duties in June and serve an unspecified probation period'.

Of course, with the benefit of hindsight, most commentators subsequently came to the conclusion that Wilf had little chance of success in this capacity, that he had inherited a form of poisoned chalice. However, given that Sir Matt was staying at the club, in some respects the appointment made a lot of sense. There was an obvious element of continuity, that Liverpool would copy with their boot room appointments in future years. Wilf had good coaching experience and had indeed been an important member of the back-room staff for Alf Ramsey's successful World Cup campaign. In some ways United were ahead of their time, the European model of a young coach and an older general manager became commonplace on the continent in later years. The only problems, though, were going to be McGuinness's lack of autonomy (particularly in transfer business), and the demarcation issue of who the real 'boss' was.

Nonetheless, there was some sense of a new start from a supporter's point of view as the 1969-70 season got underway. As had become the norm, there were no new faces for McGuinness to introduce. Amazingly, United had purchased just one player, Willie Morgan, in the last five years. This might have given me some cause for concern, but McGuinness showed an understanding of the United way, and the home-grown trio of Rimmer, Burns and Givens appeared in his first lineup. Things were not going well. After a scrappy draw at Palace, the veteran, Bill Foulkes, was horribly exposed as Southampton thrashed United in the first home game. The fixture list was not being kind to Wilf either, as the team that would be champions that season, Everton, played the Reds twice in the opening four games. The home defeat was bad enough, but there was mystification as Bobby and Denis were dropped for the return at Goodison; another defeat. For Wilf and the supporters this was a traumatic start, without a win in five opening games United were down with the deadmen. The papers were full of speculation that Wilf would be entering the transfer market to bolster his ailing squad and with his knowledge of the young England team it seemed possible that there would be an infusion of talented youth. Wilf made clear in his autobiography, in later years, that over his tenure he had identified the exciting talents of Colin Todd, Mick Mills and Malcolm Macdonald as suitable recruits. Instead, we got Ian Ure, the craggy Arsenal centre-half to relieve poor Bill Foulkes. It was not a move that quickened the pulse of the supporters, but it offered some short-term stability and kick-started a recovery as United at last began to win games.

At the forefront of this recovery was George Best. Quiet in those early dispiriting games, George hit form as he scored the only goal in United's first win of the season, and followed this up with ten goals in the next nine games. United won six of these games, and two results stood out. The five-two goal fest against Bobby Moore's West Ham had us all thinking the good times were back, as George scored twice and United played with their old attacking swagger. Doing the double over Liverpool didn't do Wilf's hopes any harm either. Willie Morgan had scored the only goal at Old

Trafford, but we were besides ourselves with joy when United thrashed Liverpool 4-1 at Anfield. The goal of the game was when George fed Bobby Charlton and his trademark screamer rocketed into the corner of the net. A lip reader, watching the goal on match of the day that night, could make out Bobby's colourful description of the goal! The morale boosting victory set up United very nicely for their semi-final with City, just four days later.

City were a very good side by 1969, for so long in the doldrums, they now appeared to have the upper hand in Manchester, as United hadn't beaten them for two seasons. The Maine Road club were a mix of locally produced players and canny bargain-priced transfer buys. They were relatively unique in that the side was totally made up of Englishmen; unusual even in those far-off days. They had caused a shock to my system by grabbing the Championship in 1968 from right under United's nose, as the Reds unaccountably lost a home game to Sunderland. It didn't seem to matter because within a couple of weeks United won the European Cup and all was right with the world again. However, a month before this semi-final they inflicted a four-nil mauling on McGuinness's team that left a certain foreboding in United hearts as they prepared for the Wednesday night game.

THE MATCH: MANCHESTER CITY 2 UNITED 1   3/12/1969

The memory of that game seemed to be in United's mind as they made a very nervous start, and it was City that dominated the opening half-hour. After just thirteen minutes United's overworked defence cracked and City went in front. Lee made a typically bustling run down the left and, after evading a couple of United tackles, sent in a fierce shot which deflected and spun high into the air. Bell, following in, met the loose ball on the half volley and crashed it past Stepney. City stayed in command and came close to increasing their lead in the minutes before halftime. It was a different story in the second half, as United, with Charlton outstanding, began to look the more likely side in what was fast developing into a pulsating contest. United now held the territorial advantage, with much of the danger to City's back line coming from Best's skilful sorties over the mud. Indeed, it was the Irishman that set up United's deserved equaliser. As Book struggled to recover, Best dribbled past him and sent an inviting pass out to Kidd on the right, who instantly pulled the ball into the penalty area where Charlton had timed his run to perfection and drove the ball beyond Corrigan. The game seemed certain to end in a draw, but then with just two minutes left City gained a vital second goal. Lee's run into the penalty area was ended by what United believed was a theatrical fall, as Ure put in a tame but desperate lunge. Lee had the Chinese sobriquet of 'Leewonpen' that season, and certainly Jack Taylor was in no doubt as he pointed to the spot. Despite all the protests, Lee kept his cool and drove the penalty past Stepney.

Despite this outcome, United continued to attack and twice came close in the frantic final seconds. Firstly, Best broke through the city rearguard and seemed certain to score until he was upended. Despite the appeals for a penalty, Mr Taylor waved play on. Seconds later, George was frustrated again as his header looked goal-bound but was cleared off the line.

So, it was a very discontented George Best that entered into an animated conversation with the referee as they left the field at full time, and as the photographer snapped his camera George knocked the ball from the referee's grasp and Jack Crompton rushed across to usher Best away.

Lee gets winner in last minutes

By ERIC TODD : Manchester City 2, Manchester United 1

Manchester United, who were beaten 4-0 by Manchester City in a League match at Maine Road a few weeks ago were in no mood to suffer another such personal affront on the same ground last night. They were all set for a draw, but a penalty two minutes from time brought City victory 2-1 in the first leg match of their Football League Cup semifinal.

City were retarded mentally and physically by these forthright methods is open to debate. The fact remained that after the interval, City, Oakes, and Booth always excepted, were anonymous.

Nothing gave greater pleasure to United's followers —and to those City partisans who were prepared to admit it —than the performance of Charlton whose distribution was, as they say, "out of this world." Best especially took full advantage of this largesse,

A UNITED TEAM IN TIME

League-Cup Semi-Final Line-up: Stepney, Edwards, Dunne, Burns, Ure, Sadler, Best, Kidd, Charlton, Stiles, Aston

There was little immediate response from the newspapers to the incident, the next day's Guardian match report didn't even mention it. However, the television cameras were there and had caught the scene, that they broadcast and focused upon. Within twenty-four hours the FA, with the referee's report in hand, decided they would launch an enquiry into the incident.

While Best and United waited for the FA enquiry to be completed, United with George in the side took on City in the eagerly anticipated second leg at Old Trafford. The evening didn't start well as City scored to take a two-goal advantage in the tie. However, United with the crowd behind them fought back in sterling fashion and Edwards and Law scored to put United ahead on the night and make the tie all square. In the closing stages with United well on top it seemed as though Wembley was beckoning for the Reds. However, with minutes remaining disaster struck as Stepney made an unnecessary attempt to save an indirect free-kick and Summerbee bundled in the rebound. Despite United's best efforts there was to be no trip to Wembley for Wilf or George, instead there remained the nervous wait for the outcome of the FA enquiry.

George Best's disciplinary record to this point was excellent, especially when one considers, as Eric Todd put it, that he 'was a genius, that suffered more than most from tough treatment'. In five seasons at United he had accrued just five bookings and a sending off in the notorious rough house that was the World Club championship match with Estudiantes. However, as United began to struggle, the weight of being United's main man seemed to increasingly weigh heavy on Best's shoulders. Duncan Hamilton, in his comprehensive biography of Best, summed up the changing landscape: 'Best had rarely got into trouble with referees before; now they were becoming regular occurrences'. More tellingly he added that the newspapers were now much more on George's case: 'He was accused of becoming whiney and brattish and spoilt, far too headstrong for his own and United's well-being'. When the FA finally concluded their enquiry and announced their sentence on January 2nd there was widespread shock as George was banned for twenty-eight days and fined £100. The severity of the sentence was without precedent and sent shock waves through the game. Eric Todd's sympathetic headline: 'Best suffers severely for foolishness' couldn't hide the fact that this was a body blow to George, Wilf McGuinnes, the club and its supporters.

Best suffers severely for foolishness

By ERIC TODD

George Best, successful business man and footballer extraordinary, has been suspended for a month and fined £100 by the FA Disciplinary Committee. United in general and Best in particular thus were in a state of confessed shock when they left Manchester for today's FA Cup tie at Ipswich. It will be interesting he suffers more than most from tough treatment by opponents—but on the whole he suffers indignity tolerably well. He has had five bookings spread over seven seasons with United; he was sent off in the World Club Championship match against Estudiantes inclined to overlook the incident or even to play it down if the game had not been televised.

Television is an inconsistent witness at football matches, recording as often as not only what it thinks the public should see. Sometimes it is not even there. My own view

Strangely enough, as soon as George played his last game before suspension against Ipswich in the FA Cup, United put together a good run of results in his absence. Undefeated in four games and with a couple of wins, the press maintained their stance that maybe United were better off without their mercurial Irishman. The insinuation was that United were showing greater harmony and teamwork without Best, and there were serious doubts that he would be recalled at the first opportunity, which was a Fourth round FA Cup tie away at Northampton. Wilf McGuinness didn't have any such doubts, describing in his autobiography the press's view as 'rubbish'. Best was recalled and the rest, as they say, is history. On a mud patch of a pitch, George handed out a soccer exhibition as he scored six times in United's 8-2 victory. John Heilpern, in the next day's Observer, concluded the debate thus: 'His unique contribution made the suggestion that United play better without him, look simply insane. To have seen Best score those six goals is to have seen genius'.

Once more a Cup, this time the high-profile FA Cup, held an opportunity for Wilf to save his season and for George to complete his medal collection. A tough quarter-final with Middlesbrough was navigated before a titanic semi-final battle with Leeds. It took three matches, including the notorious second game (subsequently made famous by Best's pre- match bedroom antics), before a single goal consigned the season to what might have been.

George Best finished the season as United's top scorer with twenty-three goals, a position he held four times between 1967 and 1972. In total he scored 179 goals for the Reds, which left him the sixth highest goalscorer in United's history. His 470 appearances for United was quite remarkable, given the premature finish to his club career. He finally left United, announcing his retirement from the game at the age of twenty-six in 1972. Although he did come back briefly during the '73-74 season and indeed played on in the game at various places until 1983. His peak years, though, were with United. During those wonderful years from 1964 we were seeing one of the greatest players in the world on a regular basis. He left an indelible memory on all of us that were lucky enough to see him play.

THE BIGGER PICTURE

Although the '69-70 season had ended in relative disappointment, Wilf McGuinness was actually promoted to official manager by the start of the '70-71 season. Again, without any player reinforcements, the side stuttered in the league, but the League Cup offered a first trophy once more. An inviting semi-final draw against third division Aston Villa was not won, and this proved too much for the board, who relieved McGuinness of his duties (as they say), four days after Christmas day in 1970.

MANAGERIAL RECORD OF WILF MCGUINNESS

	League	League Cup	F A Cup
1969-70	8th	SF	SF
1970-71	15th*	SF	

(* when dismissed)

Matches Played: 88   Wins: 36%

Most expensive signing: Ian Ure (£80.000) (But bought by M.Busby, General Manager)

Most significant youth player debut: Don Givens

DOES HISTORY REPEAT ITSELF?

Following the uniquely successful reign of Sir Alex Ferguson, Manchester United faced a similar dilemma to the Busby succession, in terms of replacing the irreplaceable. Not surprisingly, it has proved to be something of a challenge. It makes a fascinating contrast to compare this managerial process to the one that started all those years ago when Sir Matt Busby retired.

David Moyes was the man chosen to replace Sir Alex Ferguson, so in terms of chronology he is the equivalent to Wilf McGuinness. His appointment was not unlike McGuinness's, as he appeared to be the 'chosen one' of the previous manager and there was some suggestion in the media that his lack of trophies made him a lightweight for such a demanding job.

The parallels with McGuinness go deeper in that his one main opportunity of a trophy to establish his reign was the Cup. Once more it was the League Cup that offered a route to this end and what potentially was a Final with Manchester City. Despite an inviting semi-final against relegation bound Sunderland, United lost on penalties. The Champions he had inherited from Sir Alex Ferguson occasionally showed their capabilities, such as the impressive away win at Bayer Leverkusen in the Champions league. However, their progress in that competition was halted by Bayern Munich at the quarter-final stage and that, together with failing to meet the required standard of fourth and qualification for the following seasons Champions League, meant that David Moyes was sacked on April 22nd, 2014. In an echo of times past, he had lasted less than ten months in the job.

MANAGERIAL RECORD OF DAVID MOYES

	League	League Cup	FA Cup	Europe
2013-14	7*	SF	Round 3	CL QF

(* when dismissed)

Matches played: 51   Wins: 52%

Most expensive signing; Juan Mata (£37.1 Million)

Most significant youth player given debut: Adnan Januzaj

5

IN THE PICTURE

MARTIN BUCHAN

To many, Martin Buchan might be a forgotten figure in the history of Manchester United, but for most fans watching United in the 1970's, Buchan was the leading man for the Reds in those dark days of transition after Sir Matt Busby and the 'trinity' disappeared from the scene. In the picture, Buchan poses with his Cup-winning medals won with United in 1977 and Aberdeen in 1970. The point of the photograph was that his achievement was unique; he had become the only player to captain both Scottish and English FA Cup winning sides. Given the profusion of talented players that had moved south from Scotland, a traditional hot bed of player talent throughout most of the twentieth century, this statistic still surprises me. In the photograph, Martin is in his prime and had just captained United to their FA Cup Final victory of 1977, that essentially stopped Liverpool achieving the seemingly impossible 'treble'. It took another team twenty-two years to prove the impossible could be done. Once Bobby Charlton moved onto player management at Preston in 1973, Martin Buchan became my new favourite at Old Trafford. I always think of Martin Buchan not in terms of running around Wembley with the cup, but on his arrival in the troubled days of 1972.

In particular, my mind goes back to that strangest of roller coaster seasons, 1971-72, when Frank O'Farrell had just been appointed as the next manager of United.

Frank O'Farrell had succeeded Sir Matt Busby's caretaker term, and once more he was a surprise appointment. Although, as was typical of the time, there was little press speculation as to who would get the job. The plethora of literature in more recent years recognises that this was the time when United made their most concerted efforts to appoint Jock Stein from Celtic. With hindsight, many people from George Best to a range of media experts felt that 'the big man', with his tremendous success in Scotland and of course Europe, would have been the perfect fit for United. Certainly, he would have had the stature of dealing with the outsize demands of what was becoming the Old Trafford 'hot seat'. Hindsight is a wonderful thing. There is no certainty that his appointment would have worked, although in football terms it was certainly one of those 'what if' moments. It appeared that United were rebuffed, maybe something both sides regretted as Stein eventually was demoted to looking after the pools at Celtic and did venture south to an ill-fated appointment at Leeds some years later.

Anyway, it wasn't Jock but Frank that was at the helm for the start of the 1971-72 season. From a fan's perspective, Frank was a quiet, respectable and decent man, it placed him in stark contrast to his contemporaries; the flamboyant Clough and Allison, and no doubt counted for much in the United board room. I didn't really know much about him other than he was the manager of Leicester City on that May day in 1969, when United's victory had relegated his club. He had subsequently gained promotion and been a losing Cup Finalist and that appeared to be it in terms of his curriculum vitae.

If that was somewhat underwhelming, the start to this new season was not, as United under O'Farrell started the season wonderfully well, playing the best football seen at Old Trafford since 1968. It was just like the old days with the trinity, it seemed, back in full working order.

Needless to say, there had been no player recruitment and O'Farrell's only tactical change was to convert Alan Gowling, the 'galloping chip', from a forward position to midfield, with startlingly successful results. O'Farrell had been dealt a tough hand because United, due to the previous season's hooligan trouble, were forced to play their first two home matches at neutral venues. This in effect meant that United started the season with six 'away' games. Despite this they only suffered one defeat at Everton and had stylish victories over Arsenal and West Brom at Anfield and the Victoria ground Stoke respectively. In those six matches they recorded a sterling away win at Chelsea with ten men, after George Best had seen red. Denis Law, free of the knee injury that blighted his last couple of seasons seemed back to his scintillating best. He was regularly on the scoresheet and his televised trademark overhead kick goal had us spellbound, and commentator Brian Moore reaching for the superlatives. Bobby was thirty-four now, but he too seemed revitalised as he was regularly on the scoresheet as the Reds stayed with the early season leaders. It was George, though, that seemed to be in his element, as the fans chanted 'United are back'. He always seemed to save his best for London teams and I can still see in my mind's eye his glorious hat-trick against West Ham, Bobby Moore and all, as United won four-two in an exhibition of attacking football. A few weeks later George thrilled us again by scoring a barely believable goal against Sheffield United, as he dribbled from the halfway line, evading a set of wild challenges before slotting the ball past the advancing keeper and setting off mass celebrations in the stand behind the goal, where I and thousands of others payed homage to his genius. Match of the day for years afterwards used that goal in its opening sequence.

There appeared to be no stopping United, when Denis Law was injured for a crucial away derby at City an unknown junior appeared off the United youth conveyor belt, he was called Sammy McIlroy. Packed into City's old Maine Road ground, I witnessed a goalscoring debut from the Irishman, as United shared six goals in a pulsating match. Even a defeat at home to Leeds at the end of October failed to dim spirits, as United remained two points clear of the rest. Denis returned against Spurs and scored two typically audacious goals as United extended their lead at the top of the table. The game that seemed to emphasise United's resurgence was the stunning five-two victory away at Southampton at the end of November. Once more George scored a breathtaking hat-trick and the swagger and style of the performance reinforced the message that United were 'playing football the Busby way'.

Frank O'Farrell, it seemed, could do no wrong, and when United beat Nottingham Forest in early December they went five points clear at the top of the table. With the league programme almost at the halfway stage, I was able to tell myself that this wasn't a brief Indian summer for the team; United were back, what could possibly go wrong? Well quite a lot could go wrong and did go wrong as this teenage fan, dreaming of the prize to come, saw United not win another game until the start of March 1972. That was a run of eleven games where they picked up three points and plummeted from top to seventh in the league. Dispiriting does not do it justice. The wheels did not come off straight away, it was more of a gradual reality that things were not as they seemed. In December we were still playing well enough for me to decide on a trip to Stoke, where United were playing in a Brazil-like kit (maybe that's where it all went wrong!) and I was behind Gordon Bank's goals as Law's typical hanging header gained United a point. It was the new year that heralded a dreadful run of six straight league defeats. As United crashed to particularly painful defeats to West Ham and Wolves and George Best went missing, the papers were suddenly full of stories of O'Farrell's United 'crisis'. Eric Todd, still doing his stint for the Manchester Guardian, talked of the urgent need for defensive reinforcements and focusing on United's porous central defence, a problem since Busby's final seasons. It took until the end of January for United to actually lose top spot in a grim home defeat to Chelsea, Todd's guardian report said it all: 'Defensive failings are all part of the old, old story at Old Trafford, where forward flair is expected to be the compensating factor'. The nadir was reached by the thoroughly demoralising five-one defeat at Leeds. Reading the next day's newspapers didn't lighten the mood, most of them had a photograph of Sir Matt Busby and Frank O'Farrell sat together in the director's box. The Guardian once more summed up adroitly: 'If they had been attending a hanging, they could not have looked more solemn'. These were confusing and alarming times to be a United fan. The season had encapsulated the dramatic highs and lows this team were capable of. In some ways the form of the trinity and the ability to still produce some young talent lent support to the argument that a 'high-profile' manager may have guided United to safer waters and maintained their early season form. However, the club's serious lack of investment over a prolonged period had not been addressed, and the result was now glaringly obvious to this teenage United fan. So now instead of reading about actual football games I started to check out the papers' increasing fascination with transfer targets.

As February neared its end, it was clear that O'Farrell would spend, but it seemed clear that panic buys were not to be entertained, nor exorbitant fees. Of course, as United gradually moved into football's modern world it quickly became obvious that both these maxims would go out the window. On the same day that big spending Brian Clough contemplated spending £200,000 on a Leicester defender called Nish, United announced they had signed Martin Buchan from Aberdeen, for a fee of £125,000. On the day of the press release United were involved in a protracted FA Cup tie with Middlesbrough, a game they would win to reach the quarter finals. In those days before twenty-four-hour rolling sports news, transfer details were always brief and after the event, so finding out about our 'new' player was not easy. He was a young central defender, who was already captain of Aberdeen. I was impressed to see that he had already won International caps and was in fact the reigning Scottish footballer of the year. O'Farrell had travelled up to Scotland (with Sir Matt Busby) and pronounced himself 'delighted' with his acquisition, adding that Buchan was a 'skilful enthusiastic defensive player, who would be a tremendous asset to United'. The papers were quick to label him 'Scotland's Bobby Moore', no praise could be higher than that for a central defender. I studied the photograph's and Buchan looked so different to the seventies footballer with their sideburns and long hair, his short back and sides somehow spoke of his individuality. When I read that his hobbies were reading and studying foreign languages, I fully grasped his individuality, illustrated in later years when asked in the usual banal football pundit manner for a quick word, Buchan replied velocity! Tellingly, Buchan's signing broke United's internal transfer record, set ten years before when Denis Law had signed from Torino.

THE MATCH: TOTTENHAM 2 UNITED 0   4/3/1972

Martin Buchan made his debut on March 4th in a tough away game at Tottenham. His presence in the line-up didn't stop a losing run of six games becoming seven. Despite the depressing run, Buchan made an instant impression. John Arlott, writing in the Manchester Guardian, headlined his report: 'Buchan proves worthy'.

Buchan proves worthy

By JOHN ARLOTT

Tottenham H. 2, Man, Utd. 0

Two spectacular scoring shots within a minute confirmed the difference between a pair of cultured teams at White Hart Lane on Saturday. The gates were closed on the day's biggest League crowd—London's constant reaction to Manchester United—and they were given good footballing value for their money. A gusty wind and heavy

Arlott, of course, was more famous for his writing on cricket and that summer would be describing the demon bowler, Denis Lillee, of Australia, but on this occasion his purple prose focused on United's new defender. Arlott, strangely had a more fateful link to United, in that fourteen years before, as an aspiring writer for the Guardian, in response to a demand for more high-profile work he had been assigned to be the Guardian correspondent to cover United's away tie with Red Star Belgrade. At the very last minute he was replaced on the trip by the paper's senior football correspondent, Donny Davies, who of course was one of the eight journalists who lost their lives at Munich. All these years later, Arlott was in London, commenting on United's enduring appeal as the gates were closed before kick-off on a capacity crowd. Not surprisingly, United, bereft of confidence after their demoralising run, could make few chances, but were in the game until two goals in a minute to the hosts ended the contest. Buchan, though, became the centrepiece of Arlott's report. Buchan, he said: 'directed the Manchester defence with both an understanding and certainty that was impressive in a twenty-three-year-old'. Arlott continued: 'Neat in build, fast in

47

reaction and movement, shrewd in his reading of the game'. Arlott's perceptive comment on what was first sight was telling, no sentence better sums up Martin Buchan's qualities and value to United over the next eleven years. Similarly, he recognised Buchan's obvious leadership traits, qualities that would see him captain the Reds in six of those seasons, a skipper in the mould of Carey and Byrne. The reporter did add an important caveat to these leadership skills by summarising: 'He had an obvious telling effect on his immediate colleagues and if one man can resolve United's defensive problems, he might do so'. Future years would show that more than 'one man' was going to be required.

A UNITED TEAM IN TIME

League Line-up v. Tottenham: Stepney, O'Neil, Dunne, Buchan, James, Sadler, Morgan, Gowling, Charlton, Law, Best

Frank O'Farrell was in no doubt about his leadership qualities and amazingly, just four days later for his home debut against Everton, with Charlton not playing, Buchan captained the side. This is a remarkable statistic when you look back on it. That United side contained five European Cup winners and Denis Law, and yet Buchan was made skipper. United even managed to halt their losing run; the point gained in a drab nil-nil result was United's first in over two months. Eric Todd, concurred with Arlott's lavish praise, recording that Buchan 'did all that was required of him and with sufficient class to indicate that United have invested wisely'. However, Todd's previous warning that cavalier United needed to invest in defensive reinforcements was not heeded and within a week United won an unseemly transfer battle with Derby's Brian Clough and bought the Nottingham Forest winger Ian Storey Moore. United had to pay almost double Buchan's fee for the goalscoring winger and he had an instant impact, scoring five times in United's last eleven games of the season.

Unfortunately for him and United he only played a further thirty-two games before injury forced his retirement.

United limped to the end of this rollercoaster season, finishing in a disappointing eighth position in the league, and knocked out of both domestic cup competitions by O'Farrell's bogey side, Stoke City. **Martin Buchan** was established as a United captain in waiting, and would stay at the club for the next eleven years. His 456 games for the Reds placed him in eighteenth position in the club's all-time record appearances list. Captain of United for six seasons, he led them into three FA Cup finals in four seasons in the 1970's, and as the photograph illustrated, was the winning captain for United in 1977.

THE BIGGER PICTURE

Frank O'Farrell's United made a miserable start to the following season, '72-73. Three opening defeats were followed by a meagre four points from the following six games, leaving United near the bottom of the table. An increasingly desperate O'Farrell forgot about defensive reinforcements and made two speculative forward purchases, the veteran, Wyn Davies, and the third division hot shot, Ted MacDougall. Such moves did not bring about any sustained improvement and United remained perilously close to the relegation places. The humiliating five-nil thrashing away at Crystal Palace proved to be the final straw for the board, who dismissed O'Farrell on the twentieth of December 1972; the same day George Best announced his retirement from the game at twenty-six years of age.

United were back on the front page of the Manchester Guardian with a headline that called it: 'United's most momentous day since the Munich air disaster'.

MANAGERIAL RECORD FRANK O'FARRELL

	League	League Cup	FA Cup
1971-72	8th	Round 4	Round 6
1972-73	21st *	Round 3	

(*When Dismissed)

Matches played: 81   Wins: 37%

Most expensive signing: Ian Storey-Moore (£180,000)

Most significant youth player debut: Sammy McIlroy

DOES HISTORY REPEAT ITSELF?

Twelve months to the day that Sir Alex Ferguson announced his retirement, United appointed Louis van Gaal as the manager to replace David Moyes. The Dutchman was the club's first manager from outside the British Isles. At first sight, he would appear to have had little in common with Frank O'Farrell, as the Dutchman had managerial experience at a range of high-profile continental clubs, and had won many trophies including the European Cup; albeit won many years before his appointment. Perhaps the only similarity was that once more United had opted for a 'safe pair of hands' who was not initially a favourite for the job.

The Dutchman had just led Holland to third place in the World Cup, this impressive performance appeared to offset doubts about the wisdom of appointing a sixty-two-year- old to the job. He lasted marginally longer in the job than Mr O'Farrell, and did win the first silverware for the club since Sir Alex Ferguson's retirement. However, the prosaic nature of the football played by United over his two seasons, married to the availability of another manager, meant that he too was relieved of his duties in May 2016.

MANAGERIAL RECORD OF LOUIS VAN GAAL

	League	League Cup	FA Cup	Europe
2014-15	4th (CL qualify)	Round 2	Round 6	
2015-16	5th	Round 4	**WON**	CL Group stage

Matches Played: 103 (Wins: 52%)

Most expensive signing: Angel Di Maria (£59.7 Million)

Most significant youth player debut: Marcus Rashford

6

IN THE PICTURE

TOMMY DOCHERTY & JIMMY GREENHOFF

Tommy Docherty, known affectionately as 'The Doc', was United's third appointment after Busby; appointed just four days after Frank O'Farrell was sacked. The speed of his appointment suggested that this time United seemed to know whom they wanted to tackle what was becoming an increasingly difficult job. This picture, though, is taken four years after his appointment, as he beams into the camera lense next to one of his best purchases; Jimmy Greenhoff. This was a bizarre transfer as Greenhoff was something of a hero at Stoke City and seemed reluctant to sign, initially, but high winds had destroyed a stand at Stoke's ground, and this had forced the sale. It proved to be a master stroke for the wheeler dealer, Docherty, and despite the fact Greenhoff was approaching veteran status, he was to be fundamental in United's first piece of silverware since Busby's retirement.

Tommy Docherty was to some extent a risky appointment. He already had his fair share of football clubs and controversy. He would have yet more controversy at United, both whilst being manager and even outside of that position. I actually met Docherty many years after he left United, sharing a lift with him, during my Andy Warhol *fifteen minutes of fame*, after I had written a couple of books on United. I had been invited onto a sport radio phone-in, on the long defunct Piccadilly Radio. Docherty was the host, along with a disc jockey, and the programme was a forerunner of the talk radio phone-ins that now proliferate. Quite by accident, my arrival at the station coincided with the 'Doc's', and I shared a lift with him up to the recording studio. I wasn't sure what to expect, given that this was a man who had actually been taken to court by some of his ex-United players, but I found him quite charming. He was friendly and welcoming. What really shone through in my time with him was that he had an undiminished love of the game. Docherty's catch phrase on the programme was that everyone was 'entitled to their opinion', which given the plethora of tribalistic nonsense talked by the majority of callers, might have been something he regretted. Talking in the studio over twenty years after his United career had started, one was reminded of the amazing fact that this was the man who kept his job when United were relegated but had managed to lose it just after United had won that first post-Busby trophy.

I was in the crowd of 46,000 that welcomed Docherty as new manager, and United faced a difficult match with Leeds. As a fan, the glory days might have been fading fast, but the dramatic news seemed to be endless. The programme notes summed it up. The Frank O'Farrell managers' column had logically disappeared, in its place was a mournful piece from chairman Louis Edwards telling us that 'urgent action' had been required to rectify the clubs 'precarious position'. If that wasn't enough, hidden away on page eleven was a letter to the board from George Best, telling us all that he would 'not play football again'. The match was almost an anti-climax after all that, although United gained a valuable point in a one-one draw. New managerial appointments are supposed to give struggling clubs a boost, but there was no 'Doc bounce', as United went winless for another five games. Not that Docherty had been underemployed in that time, as United recruited four new players. It seemed to be a new player a day, as Graham, Forsyth, Holton and Macari joined the Reds. Docherty had been the Scotland manager, and all the new players were Scottish, as United took on a tartan tinge. However, it was my old favourite, Bobby Charlton, (playing in his last season) that scored both goals in Docherty's first win in February against Wolves. The 'new' United seemed to eventually bring about an upturn in their fortunes, as points were gathered and wins became more commonplace. It was the raw-boned giant centre half, Jim Holton, immediately a crowd favourite, that typified this new United. The crowd warmed to his wholehearted approach, as they sang: 'Six foot-two, eyes of blue, big Jim Holton's after you'. He proved his worth as the 'stopper' United had lacked for years, and as a scorer of vital goals, as United scrapped for survival. I remember the Newcastle game, which typified both attributes as United recorded a vital win in March. Firstly, he scored with a towering header. He would score three vital goals in this period, but later in the game he would see red for using the same part of his anatomy to fell Malcolm Macdonald. It was frantic stuff, but the purists would take note that United were changing their style. A good set of results at Easter made United safe, and surely better times were ahead next season.

Despite a reasonable start to the next season, it was not to be, as the '73-74 season continued the years of struggle that would culminate in relegation from division one. The fact that our old 'King', Denis Law, strangely now a free transfer offload to neighbours City, would contribute the final blow, proved the ultimate nightmare for both player and the faithful. To be at Old Trafford on that dreadful day was to witness something that had seemed to be five years in the making. With the penalty taking goalkeeper, Alex Stepney, our top scorer for much of the season, the lack of goalscoring had proved critical to United's demise. Worst still, United's desperation had gained them an uncharacteristic reputation as cloggers, something that apparently was put right by a word from Sir Matt as the season neared its end. Strangely, after previous managerial manoeuvres, Docherty's position was deemed safe, and for once the chairman's vote of confidence rang true. It would seem that he was to be given time as he rebuilt United. United's patience was rewarded the following season as they ran away with the second division title. Promotion was never in doubt, as a youthful and attractive side bolstered by just one important purchase, the talented Stuart Pearson, made the title certain by Easter.

It had seemed fitting that United's exile from the top division would coincide with me leaving my hometown of Manchester for educational purposes and ending up in Leeds, of all places. Without putting too fine a point on it, Leeds United under Don Revie were a team most football fans detested. Their ultra-professional, not to say cynical, tactics had been a byword in the game for the darker arts from their emergence as a force in the mid-sixties. The season of United's relegation had seen Leeds crowned as league champions, and now widely lauded as a good footballing side, but their previous incarnation was hard to forget. We had recently been treated to the bizarre spectacle of Leeds players running out onto the pitch with flowers and then applauding the crowd, as they worked hard on improving their image. It didn't really convince; it always reminded me of Dracula baring his lips in a smile as he sunk his teeth into his next victim. By the time I rolled up in Leeds, Revie had moved on to the England manager's job, and his replacement Brian Clough's whirlwind forty-four days had come and gone. When I went to Elland Road in October to see the Doc's youthful side beat the champions with two goals from Sammy McIlroy, I was witnessing changing times. It was the first time the Reds had beaten Leeds in years. It was to become commonplace.

The United side that had returned to the first division was literally a breath of fresh air. By November they had reintroduced two wingers to British football, and in the youthful Coppell and Hill they had two of the best in the business. With Pearson up front and a midfield made up of Macari, McIlroy and Daly, the Reds had their most attacking line up in years and were taking the top division by storm. Constantly up with the league leaders and making good progress in the FA Cup, the unlikely prospect of the famed 'double' became a real possibility by Easter. The league had been a close contest between United, Queens Park Rangers and Liverpool. Ironically, United's progress in the FA Cup - they had beaten high spending Derby County in the semi-final to reach their first FA Cup final since 1963 - adversely effected their chances in the league. Still in contention with three games of the season left, Docherty's thin squad was stretched to the limit and lost their next two games to finish third in the league. To make matters worse, they were then subject to a Cup upset as second division Southampton beat the Reds in the Final, with a goal that may not have escaped a VAR examination. Despite the anticlimactic finish, this was a season of real progress under the Doc, as United recorded their best league finish since 1968.

However, the start of the next season was disappointing, as United, unable to maintain last season's momentum and dogged by inconsistency, were not up with the early season pacesetters. Despite this, my annual October visit to Elland Road yet again yielded victory, with goals by Coppell and Daly, although it was an ugly match with confrontations on the pitch and in the stands. The win, though, was a rare highlight in a grim autumn, that saw United go five games winless after the Leeds game and drift down to fourteenth position in the league. It seemed as though the first division sides had worked out the Doc's team.

It was in the midst of this depressing run that Docherty pulled off the surprise purchase of Jimmy Greenhoff.

Greenhoff was something of an iconic figure at Stoke City, and as a thirty-year-old was in line for a lucrative testimonial, at a time when footballers were more in need of testimonials than today's players. On this basis it would seem that Greenhoff was reluctant to move, and Docherty was forced to meet him a number of times. Rather typically of the period, the fact that recent storms had destroyed a stand roof at Stoke's ground became the crucial factor in forcing the sale through. So, when Docherty and Greenhoff are seen smiling in the picture that precedes this chapter, it was the third meeting between the two, before pen was finally put to paper.

Greenhoff took a few matches to settle in, but by the turn of the year his thoughtful play and ability to hold the ball up marked him out as the focal point of a mobile attack. I was in the crowd two days after Christmas, when in the game with Everton his spectacular lob set United on their way to a resounding four-goal win. Greenhoff's arrival had proved to be the catalyst as the forwards started scoring freely and United won eight of their next ten games, culminating in a thrilling win over Manchester City. By this time United once again had Wembley in their nostrils, as Docherty tried to make good on his promise of returning the Reds to Wembley after last year's disappointment. As fate would have it, they were drawn to play last year's rivals Southampton in a fifth-round tie away at the Dell. A close game resulted in a draw and a replay at Old Trafford. I was in the seasons highest attendance as Docherty's side delighted their audience with another attacking display. The replay proved what a galvanising effect Greenhoff was having on the Doc's United, as his two goals were decisive in a two-one victory. In the first five minutes he showed what a poacher he could be, as his close-range header opened the scoring at a raucous Old Trafford. Despite Southampton's equaliser with twenty minutes left and the crowd at fever pitch, his alert anticipation and deft header settled the tie. United had moved up to fourth in the league, prompting talk of what might have happened if Greenhoff had been signed earlier, and maintained their Cup progress with a hard-fought victory over Aston Villa in the quarter final. Given my location, I was certain who United would play in the semi-final, and true enough, as I listened to the draw on the radio it was Leeds United that were drawn to play the Reds at Hillsborough.

THE MATCH: UNITED 2 LEEDS UNTIED 1 23/4/1977

Sheffield wasn't far to go to see United effectively settle the tie and guarantee their return to Wembley, inside a frantic opening fifteen minutes. It was a blustery Saturday afternoon as the teams lined up and what was noticeable was how small United looked in comparison to the giant-like Leeds outfit. However, this partly explained that decisive opening as United buzzed about their task, whereas Leeds looked ponderous in comparison. Needless to say, it was United's talisman, Greenhoff, that joyously opened the scoring. Hill's in-swinging corner was not dealt with by Frank Gray, whose hacked clearance presented the ball to Greenhoff, and a clinical finish flashed the ball past the keeper and into the top corner of the net. The goal sent the United fans wild with delight, and they roared on their favourites as they laid siege to the Leeds goal. Within minutes they had doubled the lead, as Hill's ambitious shot spun off a Leeds defender and looped across to Coppell, who sent an instant volley soaring past the Leeds keeper. That seemed to settle the nerves as United's superior teamwork kept Leeds at bay, and the veteran Stepney pulled off a couple of important saves. However, any thoughts of a relaxed finale for team and fans was interrupted when, with twenty minutes to go, Leeds gained a fortuitous penalty. Clarke's goal from the spot ensured a more nervous finish than had seemed likely after that exciting opening quarter of an hour. Now, reading the Manchester Guardian on a Monday had returned to being an enjoyable experience, and David Lacey was unstinting in his praise of United, and in particular, the role of Jimmy Greenhoff. Lacey praised United's teamwork, which he claimed was 'the essence of Manchester United's football', as he rightly emphasised that in this game 'there was only one United' (a nod to Geoffrey Green's seminal book on the club). More specifically, he pointed out that in contrast to last season, United had, 'added a wrinkle or two to their style without losing the spontaneity and openness in approach which continues to make them the biggest draw in the country'. The 'wrinkle' he was referring to was Greenhoff, who he claimed was United's 'most significant' move in years and whose influence on the tie he proclaimed with the headline of his match report; 'Pulling the strings'.

⚽⚽⚽

A UNITED TEAM IN TIME

Semi-Final line-up: Stepney, Nicholl, Houston, McIlroy, B Greenhoff, Buchan, Coppell, J Greenhoff, Pearson, Macari, Hill.

Tommy Docherty's often paraphrased mantra of your 'name' being on the cup was borne out just twenty-eight days later. Liverpool, chasing an unprecedented treble, were stopped in their tracks as United's two-one victory ensured that the club had finally won some meaningful silverware for the first time since that momentous May evening back in 1968. Naturally, Jimmy Greenhoff was the scorer of the winning goal. On this occasion he knew little about it, as Macari's hopeful shot deflected off Greenhoff's chest and sailed over the stranded Clemence and into the Liverpool net.

Jimmy Greenhoff, the catalyst of United's change of fortune during that '76-77 season, had proved to be an inspirational mid-season purchase, in much the same manner as Bruno Fernandez would transform Ole Gunnar Solskjaer's managerial season in 2020. Despite the fact that he joined the club in the year of his thirtieth birthday, Greenhoff showed an amazing durability, remaining a key component of the United attack and returning to Wembley for another FA Cup final two years later; not leaving the club until 1980. His silky skills ensured that he made and scored a lot of important goals for the club, in total playing 123 times for the club and scoring 36 goals. The classy Greenhoff remained a firm favourite of the fans, winning the club's player of the year award in 1979.

THE BIGGER PICTURE

On the surface, Tommy Docherty had the soccer world at his feet following the FA Cup final win. Having rebuilt United, he had created a youthful and exciting team that played the game the 'Matt Busby way'. In addition to the winning of silverware, there now appeared to be exciting plans on how the club could build on their success. There had been much press speculation that United would finally replace their veteran goalkeeper Stepney, with the England goalkeeper, Peter Shilton. Such a move would surely have strengthened the team and set United up for a sustained challenge for the league title. Instead, within forty-four days of United winning the Cup, Tommy Docherty was sacked, and in the autumn Shilton signed for Nottingham Forest.

The Mary Brown affair meant that once more United fans were reading the front page of the newspapers rather than the sports pages, and the fallout from the revelations meant that United sacked Docherty and started to search for their fourth manager in less than ten years. For fans of a certain vintage, Docherty's side for the last three seasons of his tenure evoke fond memories of United playing attacking football that thrilled the capacity crowds that had returned to a level not seen since the halcyon days of '68.

MANAGERIAL RECORD OF TOMMY DOCHERTY

	League	League Cup	FA Cup	Europe
1972-73 (23/12/72)*	18th		Round 3	
1973-74	21st (Rel)	Round 2	Round 4	
1974-75	Div2 (Champ)	Semi-Final	Round 4	
1975-76	3rd	Round 4	Finalist	
1976-77	6th	Round 5	**WON**	UEFA R 2

*When appointed

Matches Played: 228 (Wins: 47%)

Most expensive signing: Stuart Pearson (£200,000)

Most significant youth player debut: Brian Greenhoff, Arthur Albiston

DOES HISTORY REPEAT ITSELF?

Jose Mourinho was the manager that United had earmarked to take over from Louis Van Gaal and become the third manager after Sir Alex Ferguson. In some people's eyes, his appearance in 2016 was three years too late, as he had been widely touted for the job upon Sir Alex's retirement. In those intervening three years he had managed to win the premiership but had suffered bruising sackings at Real Madrid and Chelsea. Non the less, when he was appointed at United, it was widely seen as United spending big to ensure they had one of the world's leading managers, who had a CV to match. Although from a different age altogether, he had some similarities with Docherty, as both were controversial, high-profile managers, with a wealth of managerial experience. Although the similarity would end there, as Docherty possibly had more in common with Van Gaal (both were appointed from National team managerial positions and both were sacked after winning the FA Cup!), Mourinho was certainly entrusted with a bigger transfer kitty than any of his predecessors. His spending initially brought success, as in his first season he won the League Cup and the Europa League trophy, which ensured United returned to the lucrative Champions League. However, his second season proved strangely disappointing, despite being runners up in the League and the FA Cup. Once more December proved to be a cruel month for United managers, as that was the date, in his third season, when he was relieved of his duties following a set of poor results.

MANAGERIAL RECORD OF JOSE MOURINHO

	League	League Cup	FA Cup	Europe
2016-17	6th	**WON**	Q/F	EUROPA **WON**
2017-18	2nd	Round 5	Finalist	CL last 16
2018-19	6th*	Round 3		

(*Club position when dismissed)

Matches Played: 144 (Wins: 58%)

Most expensive signing: Paul Pogba (£89 million)

Most significant youth player debut: Scott McTominay

7

IN THE PICTURE

STEVE COPPELL

Stevie Coppell was in many ways a perfect representation of Manchester United in the late seventies. Managers may have been coming and going, but Steve was a permanent fixture racking up a club record of 206 consecutive league appearances between January 1977 and November 1981; a record that still exists to this day. An immensely popular player with the fans, he cut a different profile than your average footballer, being one of the 'university' footballers that played the game, his cool persona attracted a certain following, but it was his wholehearted application to the

Reds cause that was the basis of his popularity. The picture that opens this chapter is of a disconsolate Coppell trudging around Wembley in May 1979, following the dramatic finale of that years FA Cup Final. His expression tells the story as United came out the wrong side of a late flurry of goals that transformed an undistinguished final and placed it into the category of the more memorable; some critics even compared it to the Mathews Final of 1953. More than anything else, Steve Coppell represented the significant changes that had happened to United since the dramatic exit of Tommy Docherty and the arrival of his managerial successor, Dave Sexton. Coppell, the flying winger, had epitomised the Docherty team; the player picked out of obscurity by the legendary Jimmy Murphy, who had helped to transform United's fortunes as they returned to playing fast attacking football. Here we are two years later and now Dave Sexton, the modern coach, had converted Coppell to a withdrawn midfield role, who now combines rushing forward to scurrying back to give assistance to his defence. To be fair to the studious Sexton, it was an evolution that reflected changing tactics in the game and the number of England caps that Coppell won would suggest he made a success of the role. But from a fan's perspective, something rather crucial had changed. It was just not the same as United continued to struggle to replace the glory days of Sir Matt Busby.

Sexton had been appointed in the summer of 1977. He had for a long time been on United's radar and apparently came close to being appointed after Wilf McGuinness. He was a well-respected coach, renowned for his thoughtful approach to the modern game. More importantly to the United board, he had the reputation of being a gentleman of integrity. These were clearly values the board were desperate to achieve following the front-page headlines of a volatile summer. From my own perspective, I was still based in Leeds, and this proved to be relevant as midway through Sexton's first underwhelming season he raided the Elland Road club by purchasing the backbone of their team. I was able to follow the press on both sides of the Pennines with increasing amazement as Sexton purchased the Scottish internationals, Joe Jordan and Gordon McQueen. The reason for my amazement was that United, for the first time, were really spending big as they targeted a high-profile first division side and effectively bought their key players. However, there were mixed feelings, as these were the very players I'd seen the Doc's impish team swarm all over on the way to victory in the semi-final of '77, and many times before. What it illustrated was the change in direction the club were now taking following Sexton's faltering first campaign. It was a season that had started well but had declined alarmingly. There was to be no Elland Road victory this time, as I watched a drab draw in September. The autumn was littered with demoralising defeats, as trips to Old Trafford were no longer such joyous occasions. December summed up the fluctuations in form that often accompany managerial changes, as the old free-wheeling United tried to merge into a new more functional formation. I stood on the terraces as Brian Clough's champions-in-waiting thrashed United four-nil, but nine days later a floodlight failure at Goodison Park seemed to give us a flashback to the old days, as United recorded a six-two win, with all the Doc's heroes on the scoresheet.

It proved illusionary as United drifted towards a mid-table position, a team struggling to adapt and seriously undermined by a failure to replace the veteran goalkeeper, Stepney.

Tellingly, the Doc's side began to break up and it was a change to the role of wingers that would prove to be most significant. The Doc's side had effectively reinvented wingers, they were a throwback to fast and skilful forwards that were able to beat defenders, cross the ball and often score sensational goals. In Coppell and Hill, Docherty had two of the best in the game. Now, wingers were viewed with suspicion, potential weak points in a game that placed an emphasis on tight formation and teamwork; a winger's role now became akin to a midfielder, often with defensive responsibilities.

Steve Coppell proved very adept at these changes. Always an industrious player, he was able to shuttle forward and backwards to good effect, still able to cross and shoot but also able to help out in defence. Gordon Hill, his wing twin, did not show the same attributes, and would become surplus to requirements. For the fan on the terraces these were confusing times. Hill, still scoring his fair share of spectacular goals, was soon reunited with the Doc, now manager at Derby. To add to my bewilderment, there now started the Leeds transfer saga, so typical of every close season nowadays, but rare in those far-off days of the seventies. The Daily Express even had the novel idea of reporting on an opinion poll that it had commissioned on United supporters, asking whether they most needed a centre-half or a centre-forward. That the respondents voted in clear numbers for a centre-half was an interesting juxta position for a club that had always put a high premium on its attacking players. This seemed harsh on the popular and hardworking Brian Greenhoff, who had formed an effective partnership with Buchan, but reflected a long-held view that centre-half was a weakness that Busby had not rectified when manager. Despite the opinion poll, Sexton seemed to decide he wanted both positions filled, as in February Joe Jordan joined from Leeds, but the Yorkshire club emphasised that his Scottish compatriot would not be following. I was able to follow the story at firsthand, as the Yorkshire Post reported on Leeds digging in and McQueen apparently going on strike. This, of course, was setting a template for the modern game that would be repeated many times over; Rio Ferdinand would tread a similar path twenty-four years later. By the end of February, McQueen had been prised away and I was in the crowd in March when a towering header from him scored against West Brom, ironically it was his goal scoring that would prove more valuable to United than his defending. By the season's end, United had added their own Scottish backbone to the defence, but strangely the Buchan, McQueen partnership never really flourished.

Nothing really changed in Dave Sexton's second season other than the side continued its transformation. The addition of the workaholic, Mickey Thomas, to the side spoke volumes of the way the team were developing. The job market had opened up for me, but I stayed in Yorkshire, moving south to Sheffield. I just had time to take in one more victory at Elland Road and witness the relatively surreal occurrence of Gordon McQueen scoring the winner against Leeds. However, that was when the fun stopped as yet another autumn of inconsistency and poor results put the Reds out of Championship contention before bonfire night. It was the Christmas period that spelt out to me just how much the club were struggling, and that after just eighteen months yet more questions were being asked about the direction of the club under Sexton. I was in attendance at all three fixtures, rushing away from work to attend the first game, a grim night at Bolton. I was in a terrace that seemed to be joined onto a local DIY centre and given the paucity of United's display I might have been more profitably engaged in the store than freezing on the terraces.

Money was beginning to act as a divide between these old north-western rivals, but it mattered little this night as Bolton played all the football and ran rings around a hapless United. Frank Worthington added to the gloom by scoring a sensational individual goal that made fools of United's static defence. Boxing day brought little festive cheer as Liverpool, on the way to a decade of domination, comfortably beat United at a gloomy Old Trafford. However, it was the third game that proved most bewildering, as Ron Atkinson's skilful West Brom side inflicted a painful five-three defeat on the Reds, playing the kind of attacking football that I had always considered to be United's birth right. Things clearly were not right, and the press speculated that more managerial change was likely at Old Trafford.

Stevie Coppell kept doing his thing, first name on the managers team list, he restored some pride, scoring twice in a comfortable win at City in the new year, but by that time it was obvious that the only possible salvation for both United and Sexton would be the FA Cup.

Fortunately, they had set off in pursuit of the Cup with a sterling display against Chelsea, where Coppell won the man of the match award with a typically valuable contribution to United's three-nil win. Outjumping the giant Chelsea defence, he opened the scoring with a brave header and then he went on to make both the other goals as United ran out comfortable winners. Jimmy Greenhoff was still at the club, and he had lost none of his sharpness in front of goal by scoring the winning goals in both the fourth and fifth round ties. The FA Cup route to salvation looked more difficult when United drew Tottenham away, but brought the Londoners back to Old Trafford for a replay after a hard-fought draw. I was in a raucous full house crowd for that replay and United finally played with a mixture of fire and creativity to move into the semi-finals, but the pairing with the Liverpool machine posed a serious threat to United's progression. However, it was a spirited United side that were minutes from Wembley, leading two-one in that game, until Alan Hansen scrambled a late equaliser.

Not for the last time, Hansen proved to be less than adept at football analysis, as when he left the field he announced to the television cameras that United had missed their chance.

Naturally, United won the replay played at Goodison Park as the ageless Greenhoff stooped to head the ball past Clemence from close range. An iconic moment for United fans, and one that was all too rare in those dog days of the seventies.

THE MATCH: ARSENAL 3 UNITED 2   12/5/1979

It was a strange Cup final; in many respects a total anticlimax, as United struggled to impose their game on a more dominant Arsenal side. The fact that the Final is considered one of the more memorable Cup Final's was almost exclusively due to the dramatic finale, with three crucial goals being scored in the three minutes between the eight-sixth and eight-ninth minutes. Like a lot of the United team, Stevie Coppell had struggled in the humid heat of a Wembley May day, and it was Arsenal's Liam Brady who was the games outstanding performer. After just twelve minutes, it was the Irishman's incisive pass down the right that opened up the United defence and when the ball arrived in the penalty area, Talbot beat both Buchan and Coppell to the ball and steered in the opening goal. For a while United rallied, but they seemed to be over-reliant on the high ball towards Jordan and the giant McQueen on his forays up field. Instead, with half-time beckoning, Brady's skill seemed to decide the game, as he slalomed along the United right before popping over a delightful centre that Stapleton headed past Bailey. In the second half, United made some chances, including a snap shot by Coppell, but on each occasion the ball was directed straight at the calm and reassuring figure of Pat Jennings. With minutes left, Arsenal made the predictable move of bringing on a defender to guard their lead, but suddenly having huffed and puffed all afternoon, United burst into life and grabbed a goal back. Coppell's free kick evaded everybody in the penalty area, but when Jordan sent the ball back into the box, McQueen poked out a long leg and diverted the ball past Jennings. Suddenly, United were back in the game and now it was Arsenal who were hoofing the ball anywhere as their fans nervously whistled for the full-time whistle. Then the impossible happened, as Coppell, collecting the ball midway in the Arsenal half, slipped a delightful through ball forward to the tireless McIlroy. We watched in near disbelief, as the Irishman controlled the pass and then turned inside two challenges, before drawing Jennings forward and then slipping the ball past him and just inside the far post. Cue pandemonium, both on the pitch and in the stands, as United appeared to have saved a game that had seemed for so long to have been lost. Now with the prospect of extra time against dazed opponents, surely the Cup was coming to United. As someone has said many times over, 'football is a funny game', and to prove the point, straight from the kick-off Arsenal scored the winning goal. Most fans were still celebrating, on their feet dancing with fellow fans, as they watched in a kind of trance, as Brady once more found space, Rix crossed the ball, Bailey came to catch his centre, but as it sailed over his head Sunderland slid the ball into an empty net. Hugh McIlvanney, writing in the next day's Sunday Observer, summed up the moment in his inimitable style: 'Manchester United were entitled to believe that they had contrived a small miracle of redemption when they scored twice', but eventually suffered, 'a sickening a blow as any Cup Final losers have had to endure'.

Now all this drama brings up an important question of philosophy for the football fan, not some existential debate about the meaning of life but what is the best way to lose a Final? Is it better to accept that it's not your day and subside to that predictable two-goal loss, or to reach the high of that incredible comeback, only to have it all thrown back in your face by losing with the last kick of the game? Now, while Jean-Paul Sartre might not have spent too long on this conundrum, most fans at some point of time must attempt to grapple with this dilemma. Once you know it's not your day, you can begin to rationalise this outcome and have the time to accept the inevitable. However, when one has been in the depths of despair and then suddenly, in seconds, all hope is restored only for it to come crashing down seconds later, only a football fan can understand the philosophical imprint that can have on the psyche!

A UNITED TEAM IN TIME

Cup Final Line-up: Bailey, Nichol, Albiston, McIlroy, McQueen, Buchan, Coppell, Greenhoff, J, Jordan, Greenhoff, B, Thomas

Anyway, such philosophical discussion might go some way towards giving an explanation of **Steve Coppell**'s mood as he trudged so disconsolately around Wembley in 1979. Coppell remained a first team mainstay until November 1981, when he sustained a serious knee injury when playing for England. Three operations followed, but by 1983 he was forced to retire at only twenty-eight years of age. Despite the injured years and his premature retirement, Stevie Coppell still stands in thirtieth position in the all-time appearance list of United players, playing 396 times and scoring 70 goals.

THE BIGGER PICTURE

The '79-80 season was Dave Sexton's third year in charge of United and there were hopes that the Wembley near miss might spur United on to a meaningful challenge in the league. With the expensive acquisition of Ray Wilkins, Sexton had the perfect player to apply his methods to United and indeed improvement was forthcoming as

United finished runners up, their highest position since Sir Matt Busby had won the league in 1967.

Progress was not maintained in Sextons fourth and final season at Old Trafford. Gary Birtles, his expensive signing for that season, became the symbol of another season of struggle. Unfortunately, the striker belied that description by going twenty-five games in the league without registering a goal for the Reds. It spawned a whole series of jokes, about hostages being released from incarceration and asking had Garry Birtles scored yet! Seven straight wins at the end of the season put a glow on an undistinguished campaign, but it was not enough to save the manager who was dismissed at the seasons end. Clearly a dignified man and a thoughtful coach, he had proven once more to be the wrong man for United. The soporific football of that last season led to me taking the unprecedented step of writing to the new chairman, Martin Edwards, congratulating him on making a difficult but correct decision. My new pen pal wrote back in June 1981, telling me that he was: 'glad you are in broad agreement with what we are doing'. Nonetheless, United that summer were searching for their fifth manager in twelve years. Mr Edward's, however, had plans and told me he thought next season would prove to be: 'very exciting'.

MANAGERIAL RECORD OF DAVE SEXTON

	League	League Cup	FA Cup	Europe
1977-78	10th	Round 2	Round 4	ECWC Rd 2
1978-79	9th	Round 3	Finalist	
1979-80	2nd	Round 3	Round 3	
1980-81	8th	Round 2	Round 4	UEFA Rd 1

Matches Played: 201 (Wins: 40%)

Most expensive signing: Gary Birtles (£1.25 Million)

Most significant youth player debut: Andy Ritchie

DOES HISTORY REPEAT ITSELF?

The fourth manager to be appointed after Sir Alex Ferguson was Ole Gunnar Solskjaer. United were appointing one of their own, in that Solskjaer had enjoyed a stellar career with the club as a player between 1996 and 2007. In those eleven seasons his goals had helped the club win the Premier League title six times. Despite being used in rotation and as a substitute, Solskjaer was a prolific striker, scoring 91 goals in 235 premiership appearances.

The most memorable of all his goals was the sensational late winner against Bayern Munich in the 1999 Champions league final that guaranteed United the unique treble and Ole iconic status for evermore.

Despite such a glittering cv, there was widespread surprise when he was plucked from relative obscurity to replace Jose Mourinho, initially in a caretaker capacity in December 2018. Appointing former great players at any club is a hazardous business, and Ole's managerial qualifications for the job were questioned. Like Wilf McGuinness, he had trained United's reserves, but successful spells with Norwegian club Molde and a less successful stint with Cardiff emphasised that United were taking something of a gamble.

Initially, the results that followed this surprise move have been quite spectacular. On taking over the managerial role he became the first manager in United's history to win his first six matches; this run formed part of a sequence of ten wins in thirteen Premier League fixtures. The dramatic comeback victory in the Champions League game away to Paris st German was very much part of the clubs DNA and seemed to be central to the club making his position permanent in March 2019. Typically, once appointed, the results were less impressive.

In his first full season in charge, the COVID disrupted 2019-20 campaign, the manager continued to impress despite some inconsistent results. In the chronology of former managers, he seems to have the most in common with Wilf McGuinness. Certainly, the misfortune of losing three semi-finals in the one season is resonant of Wilf McGuinness's near misses in '69-70. However, in the modern currency his third-place finish in the League, guaranteeing Champions League participation seems to be of greater value than winning a Cup.

As with all the managers since Sir Alex Ferguson, Ole Gunnar Solskjaer has not got an easy job. In the first instance he has the impossible job of attempting to emulate the most successful manager in the history of English football. In addition to this, he is attempting to do it at a time when the owners have saddled the club with a long-term onerous debt. All this has taken place when most of the club's immediate opposition have benefited from having benefactor owners who have made significant financial investment in their own clubs. It has not been an easy task for any of his more experienced predecessors and remains a taxing conundrum for the present incumbent. Although facing an uncertain future, Ole's major achievement has been to restore the club's identity, as he has pursued a campaign that has put the emphasis back on United creating and playing their own young players and restoring United's attacking flair. For that alone, he has played an important role in the predictably difficult years following the genius of Alex Ferguson.

MANAGERIAL RECORD OF OLE GUNNAR SOLSKJAER

	League	League Cup	FA Cup	Europe
2018-19	6th*		QF	CL QF
2019-20	3rd	SF	SF	EL SF

(*Took up post 19/12/18 as caretaker and appointed permanent manager 28/3/19)

Matches played: 90 (Wins: 52%)

Most expensive signing: Harry Maguire (£78 Million)

Most significant youth player debut: Mason Greenwood

8

IN THE PICTURE

BRYAN ROBSON

It is thirty-six years since this photograph was taken and yet it feels like yesterday. It remains one of the truly iconic moments in United's history. Bryan Robson, Captain Marvel himself, launches himself at the ball to score a typically spectacular header that triggers a trademark United comeback against a star-studded Barcelona team, Diego Maradona and all. There have been a lot of glorious European nights at Old Trafford, before this under Sir Matt Busby and, after, under Sir Alex Ferguson, but this night stands comparison with any, and for those that were lucky enough to be there it felt there was never a night of greater intensity. Bryan Robson was the complete midfield player, that rarity today of being a box to box player, with endless stamina, creative in attack and yet capable of shuddering defensive challenges, with a striker's nose for goal, both spectacular long-range shots and brave headers, such as the one in the photograph. Robson was cut from the same cloth as those United heroes I had associated with the glory days under Matt Busby in the sixties and before. He was United's talisman throughout the eighties and beyond, and it was no exaggeration to claim that United's fortunes were utterly dependent upon his fragile frame. When injuries took their toll, which unfortunately from time to time they did, United's fortunes dipped. When he was on the pitch anything seemed possible, miracles were a possibility when Captain Marvel was at his best. This remarkable night in March 1984 seemed to come into that category. Sir Matt Busby, just seated away to the right of me in the main stand, said after the match: 'The game took me right back to the time we pulled back two goals against Bilbao at Maine Road for that memorable win in our first season in Europe'.

The personal history of my United support was about to come full circle. My Yorkshire exile was over, and I was back in my home town for good. It was an end to all those visits back to stand on the terraces; I was about to take up a season ticket that would propel me into the seats, an exalted position that would last till this day. However, I hadn't reached this lofty status in March '84, the game was an all ticket sell-out and despite my best efforts I was ticketless. At this point my brother, who had opened this box of United delights some twenty years before, reappeared on the night of the match, proffering two best stand seat tickets. Robbo might have been capable of miraculous deeds on the pitch, but this surprise gift seemed to have come from the heavens and wasn't without its own sense of irony. As I had become increasingly dedicated to my team over those twenty years, my brother had developed an antipathy towards 'fans' and their slavish devotions to 'their' team. It was one of life's ironies; he had opened the box for me, but had himself never been able to enjoy the treasures inside it. I could only offer sympathy to someone who would never know what it felt like to scale the emotions of all those highs, that more than compensated for the misery that would accompany any disappointments. Such a waste really!

It was a very different United now, compared to the Reds at the end of the Dave Sexton tenure. The colourful Ron Atkinson had taken over as manager, once again being something of a surprise appointment. I, of course, had been in the crowd some three years before, when his impressive West Brom side took United apart with some wonderful attacking football. That performance was probably noted by United and might have played some part in his appointment. Most importantly, 'Big Ron' as he was called was responsible for bringing his old captain, Bryan Robson, to United in October 1981. He was part of an expensive overhaul, with the accent placed firmly on attack. It was an exciting time to be a United fan, as unmistakeably quality signings were made, spearheaded by the country's leading centre-forward, Frank Stapleton, who of course had scored against United in the dramatic '79 Final. In my eyes, though, the move that typified the changing times at Old Trafford was the canny swap deal Atkinson made with Everton, as the workaholic Mickey Thomas was replaced by the buccaneering full-back, John Gidman. The ex-Everton full-back's defensive capabilities were nothing out of the ordinary, but his trademark overlapping runs gave United a new attacking dimension, and he quickly became a crowd favourite. Atkinson had also gone back to his old club to pick up the Mancunian enforcer, Remi Moses, so in no time United appeared to have a very new look. The purchase of Robson took some time, but I was in the crowd that welcomed 'Robbo' to United as he signed on the pitch for the British record fee of £1.8 million.

Atkinson was building an attractive side, and although they took some matches to gel it was clear that he now had a team that could once more challenge for domestic honours. I was in the Maine Road crowd for Robson's debut in October '81. For the only time in my life I paid the exorbitant cost of the touts' black market ticket, as the game had been sold out and I travelled over for the much-anticipated debut. They were not the safest tickets, as we were stuck, behind a goal, with a load of City fans ahead of us.

Typically, the game was an anticlimactic nil-nil draw, but one or two surging runs from Robson caught the eye and gave a foretaste of what was to come for United fans over the next thirteen seasons. United were in contention for the elusive League title throughout Atkinson's first season until a barren March and early April, when ironically, such an attacking team found goals hard to come by and meant that the Reds finished third.

Atkinson's second season saw the addition of the classy Arnold Muhren, to a United midfield of Robson, Wilkins and Moses, that had an awesome look to it. United were now the bookmakers' favourites for the title, but the side had a maddeningly inconsistent streak, which meant that damaging defeats at relegation bound Brighton, mid-table Stoke and Coventry, would eventually mean that United had to settle for third place once more. It was this season that highlighted just how important the talismanic 'Robbo' was to this United side, his absence due to injury from late February and throughout March effectively put paid to United's title hopes.

However, it was in this season that Atkinson's cavalier United side showed a propensity for Cup football, something that would go on to characterise Atkinson's tenure at United; a fact that would be highlighted by the memorable Barcelona match.

In this particular season, United would get to Wembley twice. Crucially, Robson was missing for the cruel extra-time defeat to Liverpool in the League Cup Final but scored twice in the replayed FA Cup Final against Brighton to assure United of the trophy.

It was this FA Cup victory that essentially set up the Barcelona fixture the following March. In those pre-Champions League days only a country's champions could play in the European Cup, and this meant that there were many star-studded, top-quality opponents in the other European competitions and how it became possible for United to be taking on Diego Maradona's Barcelona the following season. Europe, however, was not uppermost in the minds of the United fans at the start of the '83-84 season. Surely, if 'Robbo' stayed fit Atkinson's attractive side, now augmented by the clubs traditional ability to unearth its own talent in the shape of the phenomenal Norman Whiteside, could improve on their two third placed finishes.

Now into Atkinson's third season, United roared away to the top of the table with seven victories in their opening ten games. A fit Robson was at the heart of each encouraging display and his goals helped ease a passage through the early rounds of the European competition. However, progress was limited once more by United's characteristic inconsistency, and costly home defeats to Villa and Everton ceded league leadership to Liverpool, something of a recurrent theme for this period in the '80's.

My permanent return to my home town at Christmas coincided with the exciting news that United had drawn Barcelona in the European Cup-Winners' Cup quarter finals. Although my enthusiasm was dampened when I soon realised all the tickets were gone, but my brothers miraculous intervention had changed all that. Once more, a Robson injury layoff around Christmas had cost United momentum and points, but his return in the first months of the year coincided with some thumping wins as United maintained their position as the league's top scorers. At this time, they had once more uncovered a jewel from their youth team, as Mark Hughes started to appear in the first team. Generally, the team did well in the first leg at Barcelona, trailing for most of the game to an unfortunate Hogg own goal it looked like they would return to Manchester with just a one goal deficit to overcome. However, in the dying seconds of the game Barça, roared on by a crowd of ninety thousand, seemed to have gained a conclusive upper hand, as Rojo's rocket shot bulged the net and gave Barcelona the cushion of a two-goal lead.

✪✪✪

THE MATCH: UNITED 3 BARCELONA 0 21/3/1984

Barcelona were clearly world class opponents, with a backbone of top-quality players they were augmented by one of the world's greatest players, Diego Maradona, and the classy German midfield orchestrator, Bernd Shuster. Masterminded by the Argentinian World Cup winning manager, Cesar Menotti, not one pundit gave United a chance of overturning the match deficit. Nonetheless, it was United's first proper European night since the halcyon days of the late sixties, and there was palpable excitement among the fans, both in the walk to the stadium and more particularly by the tumultuous atmosphere inside the ground. Although there had been many exciting European nights before, and of course there were going to be countless ones in the future, many United fans believe that the atmosphere in the theatre of dreams that night has never been bettered. There was some expectancy of what might be possible, but my pragmatic side came to the fore as I realised that a Barça away goal would in all likelihood finish the tie. After United's initial surge, Barça's neat possession play seemed to set the tone of what was to come, as United just had Whiteside's speculative shot to show for the first twenty minutes of endeavour. But then it happened, as halfway through the half, Robbo changed the complexion of the tie and set up the excitement to come. Wilkins' in-swinging corner had been flicked on by Hogg and Robson, in typical fashion, had anticipated perfectly to head in at the far post. Despite the pandemonium in the ground, Barça kept their calm and played out the rest of the half with relative ease, although there was a sense that Robbo had exposed a weakness that could be exploited again.

The half-time talk was all about how Moses was keeping Maradona quiet and the fact that this game could be won. Five minutes into the second half, Barcelona's nonchalant possession game caught them out, as under pressure from a rampaging United they gave the ball away and United made them pay. Victor's panicky back-pass towards the goalkeeper, Urruti, saw the keeper scuff his clearance under pressure from Whiteside and when Moses returned the ball into the penalty area the goalkeeper fumbled Wilkins' shot, and Robson was alert once more to sweep the ball in from close range. Captain Marvel wasn't done, as before we had regained our seats with Barça rocking, Robson's swerving long-range pass beat Barcelona's offside trap releasing Albiston down the left wing, his centre to the far post was headed down by Whiteside straight to Stapleton, who rammed the ball in from close range; cue pandemonium! The goal was scored just in front of us and brought everyone to their feet in a surge more commonplace in the terraces. The bloke in front of me, who had just settled down for a second-half pint of beer, was covered in the stuff, but didn't seem to mind. It left a tense thirty minutes that United and their fans had to now endure as a Barça goal would change a night of glory to one of killing anticlimax. Maradona made a couple of twisting runs but seemed strangely muted, and the main danger came from Schuster, who had two shots that were inches wide of both posts. In football however, some things are destined to be and it began to dawn on me that this was United's night. As the referee blew his whistle Ron Atkinson did a jig on the touchline and the crowd invaded the pitch to carry Bryan Robson shoulder-high from the arena and complete one of United's greatest nights.

✪✪✪

A UNITED TEAM IN TIME

European Cup Winners' Cup, Quarter-Final Line-up: Bailey, Duxbury, Albiston, Wilkins, Moran, Hogg, Robson, Muhren, Stapleton, Whiteside, Moses.

Bryan Robson stayed on for another ten seasons at United and with 461 appearances and 99 goals he remained a key player for the Reds throughout. Despite the ravages of multiple injuries, he remained an inspirational captain that led by example and other triumphs awaited in the years ahead that would reward the player's loyalty. He would become the first United captain to skipper the Reds to three FA Cup Final successes and would lift the European Cup Winners' Cup as United's victorious captain. Despite a season long battle with hamstring problems, he was in the side as United finally won their first League title since Sir Matt Busby in 1993. Nothing was more appropriate to this and many other United fans than to see 'Robbo' join Steve Bruce to jointly raise the new Premier League trophy, to end that twenty-six-year wait.

THE BIGGER PICTURE

United's dubious reward for their famous victory over Barcelona was to play Juventus in the semi-final, to further emphasise what a strong competition this was. The Italian side was largely made up of the World Cup winning Italian side, and once more had the world class additions of Michel Platini and Zbigniew Boniek. The fact that Platini was in the middle year of his hat-trick of Ballon d'Or awards, gave a taste of what United were up against. It also emphasised a recurrent theme for United in all my years of supporting them, and that was the myth that as one of the world's most famous clubs they could purchase any player they liked. This was never the case then or now, more often than not the clubs with generous benefactors as owners were in Spain and Italy, and as with Platini and lots of 'stars' in the years ahead, this is where the players went. United's big achievement was to hold on to their great players, whether they were Best in the sixties or Giggs in the nineties; in 1984 the hot property was Bryan Robson. From March onwards the media told us that we wouldn't have Captain Marvel for much longer, as Italian gold would lure our talisman away.

Juventus were not going to get first-hand evidence of his talents as, almost predictably, injury meant he missed both semi-final ties and it was an understrength United side that succumbed to Juventus, albeit by a single goal overall and that scored seconds from the end of the game.

This disappointment in Europe was mirrored by a faltering finish in the league that saw United finish fourth. Instead of Bryan Robson leaving United for Italy it was Ray Wilkins, although Atkinson replaced him with the effervescent Gordon Strachan to bolster United for his fourth season in charge. Once more United were in contention for the League title until an Easter fade out of costly draws ruined their chances. Again, the FA Cup proved to be a compensation as their ten men beat Everton courtesy of a delightful Whiteside goal. Ron Atkinson's last full season in charge proved to be an apposite summary of his time at the club, as the side's attacking play provided a high, but the end product was something of an anticlimax. After nearly twenty years of waiting for the first League title since Sir Matt Busby, the moment seemed at hand, as the Reds, playing superlative attacking football, swept all before them as they opened the season with ten straight wins and went sixteen games before tasting defeat in November. Quite remarkably, from this highpoint the side plummeted with a series of defeats and draws that eventually saw them lose the top spot and ultimately finish fourth. Predictably, this horrendous run coincided once more with a long lay-off for Robson, as his injury jinx returned. This combined with the mysterious mid-season news that we wouldn't have Mark Hughes next season, as he was being sold to Barcelona, totally deflated this and many other United supporters.

Atkinson rather tarnished his impressive buying record with a series of hasty purchases that the next season saw the forward line led by the underwhelming combination of Terry Gibson and Peter Davenport. The writing was on the wall at the start of the '86-87 season for Ron Atkinson as United, without Robson - this time injured on England duty - lost their first three league games. It was a United that now seemed strangely dull and lacking in confidence, and a four-one League Cup defeat at Southampton proved to be one of those familiar feelings of a defeat too far, as Big Ron was sacked forty-eight hours later. My old pen pal, Mr Edwards, commented that: 'In light of the team's poor performances over the last twelve months' and in the 'best interests of the club and the fans' the decision to replace Atkinson had to be made. This time United seemed to know who they wanted to replace him with, despite press speculation linking Terry Venables with the job, Alex Ferguson, the Aberdeen manager being appointed manager twenty-four hours later. My only sighting of Alex Ferguson had come four years earlier, when I caught some live television footage of the end of the Scottish Cup Final. Aberdeen had won the Cup beating Rangers, but Ferguson, interviewed at the end of the match was going apoplectic about their performance, you couldn't mistake the intensity of a born winner. The Scotsman had managed to break the Celtic-Rangers duopoly of power in Scottish football. That, together with his impressive achievement of winning the European Cup winners' Cup with unfashionable Aberdeen, marked him out as a man with a high-quality cv, and I was pleased with the appointment.

Ron Atkinson's team in the end proved to be too inconsistent to wrestle the title from Liverpool, who won the League title four times in Atkinson's five full seasons. Bryan Robson was his gift to United fans, and it was one that would keep giving long after he had left. Nonetheless, two major trophies, a top four finish in each of his five completed seasons and bringing back those exciting European nights exemplified by the Barcelona Cup tie, marked Atkinson out as clearly the most successful of Sir Matt Busby's immediate successors.

MANAGERIAL RECORD OF RON ATKINSON

	League	League Cup	FA Cup	Europe
1981-82	3rd	Round 2	Round 3	
1982-83	3rd	Finalist	**WON**	EUFA Rd 1
1983-84	4th	Round 4	Round 3	ECWC SF
1984-85	4th	Round 3	**WON**	EUFA Rd 4
1985-86	4th	Round 4	Round 5	
1986-87	11*	Round 3		

(* When dismissed)

Matches played: 292 (Wins: 50%)

Most expensive signing: Bryan Robson (£1.5 Million)

Most significant youth player debut: Norman Whiteside, Mark Hughes

9

WHAT CAME NEXT

IN THE PICTURE

Schmeichel
Parker
Irwin
(Sharpe)
Bruce
Pallister
Keane
Kanchelskis
(McClair)
Ince
Cantona
Hughes
Giggs

It took a little time, but the wait was worthwhile.

The above thirteen players were United's FA Cup Final line up in 1994, by beating Chelsea four nil in the final they won the coveted double of the FA Cup and Premier League title.

It was eight years after Alex Fergusson had taken over as manager and these two trophies brought his tally to eight, there were many more to come.

SOURCES & BIBLIOGRAPHY

The vast majority of this book is based on my own trips to the 'Theatre of Dreams' and further afield, and my own collection of memorabilia and recollection of events.

However, I am indebted and acknowledge the following sources:

Acknowledge and thanks from many years ago to Manchester Central Library and the John Rylands University Library, for access to their Daily Mail collection.

Acknowledge Newspapers.com regarding access to copies of the old Manchester Guardian Newspaper.

Acknowledge Manchester United Football Club, and the following copies of the United Review match programmes:

1964, 30 March v Fulham

1964, 13 April v Sheffield United

1971, 2 October v Sheffield United

1972, 23 December v Leeds United

1977, 5 March v Manchester City

1978, 30 December v West Brom

1984, 21 March v Barcelona

Bibliography

Barclay, P: Sir Matt Busby, The man who built a football club (Ebury Press, 2017)

Brown, J: The Matt Busby Chronicles, Manchester United 1946-69 (Desert Island 2004)

Cawley, S: United, Manchester United in the FA Cup (Champion 1994)

Cawley, S, James, G: The Pride of Manchester (Polar 1991)

Crick, M, Smith, D: Manchester United; Betrayal of a Legend (1989)

Charlton, R: Book of Soccer (Cassell, 1960)

Charlton, R: The Autobiography, My Manchester United Years (Headline, 2007)

Coppell, S: Touch and Go (Willow 1985)

Dunphy, E; A Strange Kind of Glory, Sir Matt Busby and Manchester United (Heinemann 1991)

Dykes, G: The United Alphabet, Complete who's who of Man United (ACL Polar 1994)

Green, G: There's Only One United (Hodder-Stoughton 1978)

Hamilton, D: Immortal, Approved Biography George Best (Century 2013)

Law, D: An Autobiography (Queen Anne Press 1979)

McGuinness, W, Ponting, I: Wilf McGuinness Manchester United Man and Babe (Know The Score 2008)

Meek, D: The Manchester United Football Books 1-9 (Stanley Paul 1966)

Morrison, I, Shury, A: Manchester United, A Complete Record (Breedon 1990)

Tossell, D: Tommy Doc (Mainstream 2013)

Internet Sources: MUFCinfo.com

Last but not least, a thank you to my brother Ray and all those Football Annuals entitled: The Big Book of Football Champions. I dedicate this book to you. After all, you were the man who opened up this box of treasures.

ABOUT THE AUTHOR

Steve Cawley is Manchester born and bred and started supporting United in the mid-sixties. He became a league match ticket holder in 1985 and a full season ticket holder in 1992 (a good year to make that transition). He remains a season ticket holder to this day, but for obvious reasons has not been able to attend the 'Theatre of Dreams' since March 2020.

A former sixth form tutor, Steve had previously written two books on Manchester United.

In recent years he has written three books on Horse Racing, but he has now returned to his first sporting passion; football, and more particularly Manchester United.

Printed in Great Britain
by Amazon

73570686R00052